Landmarks of world literature

Miguel de Cervantes

DON QUIXOTE

D0870565

Landmarks of world literature

General Editor: J. P. Stern

MIGUEL DE CERVANTES

Don Quixote

A. J. CLOSE

Department of Spanish,
University of Cambridge

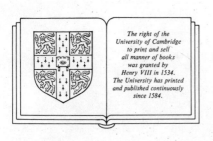

The right of the
University of Cambridge
to print and sell
all manner of books
was granted by
Henry VIII in 1534.
The University has printed
and published continuously
since 1584.

CAMBRIDGE UNIVERSITY PRESS

Cambridge
New York   Port Chester   Melbourne   Sydney

Published by the Press Syndicate of the University of Cambridge
The Pitt Building, Trumpington Street, Cambridge CB2 1RP
40 West 20th Street, New York, NY 10011, USA
10 Stamford Road, Oakleigh, Melbourne 3166, Australia

© Cambridge University Press 1990

First published 1990

Printed in Great Britain at the University Press, Cambridge

British Library cataloguing in publication data

Close, A.J.
Miguel de Cervantes: Don Quixote – (Landmarks of world
literature)
1. Fiction in Spanish. Cervantes Saavedra, Miguel de,
1547–1616. Don Quixote – Critical studies
I. Title II. Series
863'.3

Library of Congress cataloguing in publication data

Close, A. J. (Anthony J.), 1937–
Miguel de Cervantes, Don Quixote / A. J. Close.
        p.   cm. – (Landmarks of world literature)
Includes bibliographical references.
ISBN 0 521 32802 0 – ISBN 0 521 31345 7 (Pbk.)
1. Cervantes Saavedra, Miguel de, 1547–1616. Don Quixote.
I. Title. II. Series.
PQ6352. C615 1990
863'.3 – dc20   89–22287   CIP

ISBN 0 521 32802 0 hard covers
ISBN 0 521 31345 7 paperbacks

Contents

Preface

References to the text of *Don Quixote* are based on the edition
by Luis Andrés Murillo, 2 vols., Madrid, 1978. References to
Part and Chapter are given as: *DQ* I (or I), 28; references to
volume and page have the form: i, 344. References to modern
critical works appear thus in the text: ([author's name] [date]),
or in some readily intelligible variant on that pattern. Full bibliographical details are supplied in the 'Guide to further reading' at
the end of the book. Translations into English of Cervantes's text
are my own. For that reason, and because the published English
translations are numerous and readily available, I have not considered it useful to give page references to any one of them in
particular. I trust that the citation of Part and Chapter numbers
will be sufficient help to non-Hispanists in locating quotations. I
should like to express my thanks to Professor J. P. Stern, the
general editor of this series, for his meticulous and incisive comments on my manuscript for this book.

Chronology

	Cervantes's life and works	Contemporary events
1547	Born at Alcalá de Henares to Rodrigo de Cervantes, a surgeon, and Leonor de Cortinas	Death of François I and Henry VIII; Charles V's victory over Protestant princes at Mühlberg; Rabelais, *Fourth Book*; Michelangelo directs work at St Peter's, Rome; end of first session Council of Trent
1548		Robortello's commentary on Aristotle's *Poetics*
1550		Ronsard's *Odes*; Palladio, Villa Rotunda, Venice
1553		Accession of Catholic Queen Mary of England, who marries Philip of Spain (1554) and repeals Henry VIII's Act of Supremacy
1554		*Lazarillo de Tormes*; Titian, *Danae with Nursemaid*; Bandello, *Novelle*
1555		Smithfield Fires, burning of English Protestants
1556		Abdication of Charles V; accession of Philip II
1557		Spanish forces defeat French at battle of St Quentin

1558	Accession of Elizabeth I of England, who reinstates Act of Supremacy; discovery of Protestant cells at Valladolid and Seville
1559	Montemayor, *La Diana*; first Spanish Index; Calvin's *Institutes of the Christian Religion*
1561	Scaliger, *Poetics*
1562	St Teresa founds Convent of St Joseph in Avila; outbreak of Civil War in France between Huguenots and Catholic Guise faction, continuing intermittently until 1598
1563	Close of Council of Trent; construction of palace of El Escorial begins
1565	Malta withstands Turkish siege; *Life* of Benvenuto Cellini completed
1567	Palestrina, *Missa Papae Marcelli*
1568	Duke of Alba's repression of Calvinism in Netherlands provokes Eighty Years War; execution of Counts Egmont and Hoorn in Brussels
	Having studied at López de Hoyos's academy in Madrid, writes verses on death of Philip II's wife, Isabel de Valois

1569	Wounds Antonio de Sigura in a duel? Goes to Rome, enters service of Cardinal Acquaviva	Revolt of *moriscos* in province of Granada
1571	Aboard the galley *Marquesa*, fights valiantly in sea battle of Lepanto against Turks, 'the most glorious occasion seen by centuries past or present or to be seen in those to come'; is wounded and maimed in the left hand	
1572	Involved in naval expeditions to Navarino and (1573) Tunis	Luis de León's trial by the Inquisition; massacre of French Huguenots on eve of St Bartholomew's Day
1573		Tasso, *Aminta*
1575	Returning from Naples to Spain by sea, is captured by Berber corsairs and taken to Algiers; during captivity (until 1580) makes four escape attempts; his resolution recorded in Diego de Haedo's *History of Algiers* (1612), which corroborates the Captive's story in *DQ* I, 39–42; King Hassan Pasha's clemency towards him has prompted speculation about a possible homosexual liaison	Tasso, *Jerusalem Liberated*
1576		Sack of Antwerp by Spanish troops; Titian, *Pietà*; Bodin, *Six Books of the Republic*

1577		St Teresa writes *The Abodes*; El Greco begins activity in Toledo; Sir Francis Drake circumnavigates globe
1578		King Sebastian of Portugal killed at Battle of Alcazarquivir; St John of the Cross writes his *Spiritual Song of Love*; Ronsard, *Sonnets for Helene*
1579		Formation of United Provinces in Netherlands
1580	Ransomed by a Trinitarian friar; returns to Madrid; literary activity as poet and dramatist until 1587; according to the prologue of his *Eight Comedies and Eight Farces* (1615), he wrote some twenty to thirty plays in this period, of which only two survive	Philip II annexes Portugal
1581	In Portugal at court of Philip II; is entrusted with secret commission to Oran	
1582	(to 1584 approx.) Liaison with Ana Franca de Rojas; birth of Isabel de Saavedra; friendships with well-known poets in Madrid and composition of laudatory sonnets for their works	Fernando de Herrera's poems published
1583		Luis de León's *Name of Christ*

1584	Marries Catalina de Salazar	Giordano Bruno, *On The Infinite Universe*; completion of El Escorial
1585	Publishes his pastoral romance *La Galatea*; lives with Catalina in Esquivias (province of Toledo), commuting to Madrid	Queen Elizabeth sends troops to aid Dutch rebels; outbreak of war of succession in France; Veronese, *The Triumph of Venice*
1586		El Greco, *The Burial of Count Orgaz*
1587	Departs for Seville; begins activity as commissioner of supplies for Armada expedition; end of first phase of literary career	
1588		Defeat of Spanish Armada; Montaigne, *Essays*
1589		Assassination of Henry III of France; accession of Henry of Navarre; Spenser, *The Faerie Queene*
1590	Applies to Council of the Indies for employment in America in recognition of his military services; request refused: 'let him seek preferment over here'	Revolt in Aragon; Christopher Marlowe, *Tamburlaine the Great*; Sir Philip Sidney, *Arcadia*; translation into Spanish of León Hebreo's *Dialogues of Love*; Guarini, *The Devoted Shepherd*
1592	Briefly imprisoned in Castro del Río on order of magistrate of Ecija, alleging illegal sale of wheat; released on appeal; contract with Rodrigo Osorio to write six plays	Tintoretto, *Last Supper*

1593		Marlowe, *Edward II*
1594	Obtains commission to collect tax-arrears in province of Granada	*Satyre Ménippée*; Henry IV enters Paris; 'Paris is well worth a mass'
1595	Bankruptcy of Sevillian banker with whom he had deposited tax revenues	Sidney, *Apology for Poetry*
1596	Writes burlesque ode on belated liberation of Cádiz	Sack of Cádiz by Earl of Essex; López Pinciano, *Ancient Poetic Philosophy*
1597	Due to auditors' error, imprisoned in Seville for shortfall in tax-moneys due to the Treasury; in this internment *DQ* was supposedly engendered	Third bankruptcy of Philip II
1598	Writes burlesque ode on Philip II's funeral monument in Seville, later citing it as 'principal honour of my writings'	Death of Philip II; accession of Philip III; rise to power of Duke of Lerma; peace of Vervins with France; restoration of French monarchical authority and economy under Henry IV; Caravaggio, *Cycle of Life of St Matthew* (to 1601)
1599		Outbreak of plague in Spain; Mateo Alemán, *Guzmán de Alfarache* Part I; (to 1608) period of composition of Shakespeare's major tragedies
1600	About this time, departure from Seville and beginning of second phase of literary career	Edition of Victoria's music; Charron, *Concerning Wisdom*; Malherbe, Ode to Marie de Médicis; Giordano Bruno burnt in Rome

1601		Transfer of Spanish court to Valladolid
1602	Tangles with Treasury over missing tax-moneys; busy in composition of DQ	Campanella, *The City of the Sun*
1603		Death of Elizabeth I; accession of James I; Barclay, *Euphormio*
1604	In Valladolid; pre-publication references to *DQ* by Lope de Vega (slighting) and López de Ubeda (laudatory)	*Guzmán de Alfarache* Part II; First Part of Comedies of Lope de Vega; approximate date of composition of Quevedo's *The Sharper*
1605	Publishes *DQ* I; re-edition in Madrid; pirate editions in Lisbon and Valencia; Don Gaspar de Ezpeleta wounded outside his house in Valladolid, and he and his family accused of sexual immorality; Don Quixote and Sancho appear as carnival figures in popular festivites	Gunpowder plot by English Catholics to blow up Houses of Parliament; (to 1608) Quevedo writes the first of his *Visions*; Vauquelin, *Art of Poetry*
1606	About this time, composition of *The Dog's Colloquy, The Illustrious Scullery Maid, Licentiate Glass* (novelas), and appearance of two earlier novelas, *Rinconete and Cortadillo* and *The Jealous Extremaduran*, in a miscellany compiled for the Archbishop of Seville; (to 1607) moves back to Madrid	Court returns to Madrid

1607	Thomas Shelton translates *DQ* 'in the space of forty days'	Monteverdi, *Orfeo*; landings at Jamestown, Virginia
1608	Third edition of *DQ* from press of Juan de la Cuesta in Madrid	D'Urfé, *Astraea*; Champlain founds Quebec
1609	Joins Congregation of Slaves of Blessed Sacrament, along with other men-of-letters; attendance at literary academies in Madrid; estrangement from his daughter Isabel after her marriage to Luis de Molina; Richer's French version of excerpts from *DQ*	Twelve Years truce between Spain and United Provinces; decree of expulsion of Spanish *moriscos*; Lope de Vega reads his *New Art of Making Comedies* to a Madrid academy; François de Sales, *Introduction to the Devout Life*
1610	Disappointed in hopes of accompanying retinue of Count of Lemos to Naples; composes *The Little Gipsy Girl* (*novela*); (about now) at work on *DQ* II and *Persiles*	Galileo publishes first major astronomical observations; Ben Jonson, *The Alchemist*, which mentions *DQ* in Act IV
1611		Authorised Version of Bible in English; Donne, *Anniversaries*
1612	European diffusion of *DQ* I marked by Shelton's English translation	Góngora's major poems circulate in Madrid

1613	Publication of *Exemplary Novels*; dedication refers to Count of Lemos's patronage; becomes novice of Franciscan Tertiaries	(to 1615) Rubens, *The Toilet of Venus*
1614	*Voyage to Parnassus*; Avellaneda's *El Quijote*; Oudin's French translation of *DQ* I	Webster, *The Duchess of Malfi*
1615	Publishes *DQ* II and *Eight Comedies and Farces*; moral approbation preceding *DQ* II by licentiate Márquez Torres contrasts Cervantes's poverty and low status in Spain with his high reputation in France: 'Does Spain not enrich such a man and maintain him from the public purse?'	Harvey's discovery of circulation of blood
1616	Dedicates *Persiles* to Count of Lemos; mentions works unfinished at death, including *La Galatea* Part II and *Weeks in the Garden* (probably a collection of *novelas*). 'Farewell jests, farewell witticisms, farewell merry friends, for I am dying and hoping soon to see you happy in the life to come.' Dies on 22 April.	Death of Shakespeare; rise to power of Cardinal Richelieu; Aubigné, *Tragiques*
1617	Posthumous publication of *Persiles y Sigismunda*; French translation of *Exemplary Novels*	
1618		Start of Thirty Years War in Europe; fall of Duke of Lerma; Vanini, *De admirandis*

Chapter 1

Don Quixote's *premises, structure and major themes*

Critical approaches; Background; Cervantes's motives

Don Quixote, in basic conception, is a parody of Spanish romances of chivalry. It concerns an *hidalgo*, a member of the minor gentry, from a village somewhere in La Mancha. His life-style, described on the memorable opening page, conforms to that of a familiar type, associated with threadbare frugality, hunting, the relics of honourable ancestry, parochial seclusion. In short, a very prosaic backdrop for the delusions of grandeur about to fill the stage. La Mancha is the vast, featureless plain, scorchingly hot in summer, which occupies the plateau of south-eastern Castile. This *hidalgo* was an addictive reader of chivalric romances; and they took such a grip on his fantasy that he came to believe that they were historically true and that he could become a knight errant such as they depict, with all the ensuing glory and perquisites. With Sancho Panza as his squire, he rides through the countryside in search of adventure, interpreting each commonplace encounter that befalls him as one of the marvellous adventures in chivalry books. From the resulting merry confusions Cervantes has built not just a great work of comedy – parody is too narrow a term – but a novel which would appear a quasi-sacred precursor to the German Romantics and the leading nineteenth-century novelists. For Spanish intellectuals since the mid-nineteenth century it has enshrined the essence of the national culture.

The modern era has tended to convert *Don Quixote* into myth, appropriating the myth's meaning to its immediate concerns (Close 1978). This has been as true of academic critics, despite

1

their commitment to the recovery of historical context, as of novelists, poets, aestheticians, and philosophers, who feel that commitment less. The two most influential interpretations of *Don Quixote* in this century, by Ortega y Gasset (1914) and Américo Castro (1925), treat it as a supremely lucid and poised master-piece, which anticipates the secularism, ambiguity, and relativity of the modern era, reflected in the modern novel. This approach was motivated by the tacit urge to salvage from the seemingly hidebound culture of Counter-Reformation Spain an outlook and set of values prophetic of a new Spain destined to emancipate itself from the traditions of the old. The approach continued a custom, established by the German Romantics, of regarding Cervantes as an artistic colossus, who serves as a bridge between one historic era and another. This notion has not lost its grip in recent times. Thus, for Foucault (1970), *Don Quixote* symbolises the collapse of the Renaissance world-order and its replacement by that of the Classical age. Spitzer, in a seminal essay clearly influenced by Romantic concepts of irony (1948), takes the novel as a glorification of the artist, who surveys the interplay of human 'perspectives' with God-like detachment. On the threshold of the modern era, it achieves a never-to-be-repeated balance of scepticism and faith. A long line of Spanish critics, from Menén-dez Pelayo (1905) onwards, treats Cervantes as a sympathetic mediator between Spain's chivalric ethos and the modern age, mocking the former's excesses but finding a form in which to perpetuate its essence.

In attributing this forward-looking attitude to Cervantes, the critics have found difficulty in reconciling it with Cervantes's explicit ideology, which accords with the intellectual premises of his age. The lack of alignment tends to be explained away, with unsatisfactory circularity, as a symptom of his congenital ambi-guity or 'perspectivist' cast of mind. The reverential attitude to Cervantes is responsible for a related falsification: it tends to veil *Don Quixote's* essential nature as a work of comedy; and this results in a lessening of understanding and, even more unfortu-nately, of enjoyment. Those who have resisted the tendency to update *Don Quixote's* meaning (e.g. Russell 1969; Close 1978) have tended to do so from the viewpoint of literary or intellectual history. There is thus a gap in Cervantine criticism waiting to be filled. To do so adequately in a brief book aimed at the general reader is beyond my aspirations; I simply intend to offer a succinct interpretation of some central features of Cervantes's narrative art in *Don Quixote*, which takes account of their complexity while avoiding the above-mentioned misalignment. In the two main chapters of this book I consider, first, the novel's organising themes and principles in general, and secondly, the development of Don Quixote's and Sancho's personalities.

Amadís de Gaula, published in 1508, is a late, sophisticated offshoot of the corpus of Medieval prose romances – most notably, the monumental *Lancelot* (France, early thirteenth century) – celebrating the deeds of King Arthur and his Round Table. Deservedly popular in Spain for over two centuries, it generated a wave of sequels and imitations. The addicts of this literature comprised all classes: illiterate reapers at harvest time (see *DQ* I, 32), hard-bitten *conquistadores* who remembered the romances when naming parts of America, the adolescent Teresa of Avila, the great dramatist Lope de Vega. It dressed up the medieval code and practice of chivalry in fabulous garb: unremittingly marvellous adventures in a largely lengendary setting of forests, palaces, castles, tourneys, with a cast of giants, enchanters, damsels-in-distress, dwarfs, princesses, and knights whose qualities of beauty , bloodthirstiness, chivalry and so forth are invariably superlative. The moral/religious symbolism which gave serious purpose to the *Lancelot* is largely lost. Supporters of the Spanish romances could claim that they offered a mirror of true chivalry; yet, as the innkeeper's family artlessly testifies (*DQ* I, 32), the escapist inducements of violence, sentimentality, and consummated passion were more potent reasons for their success.

Throughout the sixteenth century, moralists and divines condemned the romances for their immorality, inplausibility, lack of elegance and learning; and in the second half of it, the combined influence of the Council of Trent and neo-Aristotelian poetic theory gave this criticism a sharper edge. The assembly of bishops and theologians who met at Trent to formulate Catholic doctrine in response to Protestantism, and to launch the Roman Church's own reform, called on the collaboration of literature and the arts. Simultaneously, the Renaissance literary theories based on Aristotle's *Poetics* offered literature an intellectual stiffening and status which complemented its newly acquired moral commitment. Cervantes's opposition to the romances is grounded on neo-classical principles and an ideal of what a long prose romance should be; they are formulated by his spokesman, the Canon of Toledo, in Part I, Chapter 47. Towards the end of his career he fulfilled the ideal by writing *Persiles y Sigismunda*, an epic tale of pilgrimage to Rome by two chaste, faithful lovers. It is piteous, grave, and lofty in tone, ingeniously labyrinthine in plot, deeply religious, exemplary of man's relation to Providence, written according to Aristotelian epic theory and modelled on Heliodorus's *Aethiopic History* (c. AD 250). Cervantes probably judged it his masterpiece. The interpolated tales in *Don Quixote* Part I are somewhat similar to *Persiles* in character. They represent the literary species – the romantic *novela* or episode – that Cervantes cultivates assiduously throughout his career. Integral to it are peripeties and crises which imperil or save love, life and honour: capture by pirates, shipwrecks, escapes; compromising flights from home by girls pursuing or pursued; providential reunions and wondrous recognitions. The tone is sentimental and decorous, the status of the principals genteel, the discourse courtly and rhetorical; the appeal to pathos is reinforced by the focus on women's experience of the sweet agonies of pre-marital love. The exemplary dénouements, brought about by reasoned goodwill rather than violence, feature family reconciliations, contrite villains, the prospect of marriage: in short, a middle-class ethic for middle-class characters.

The cornerstone of Cervantes's literary theory is the idea that aesthetic pleasure depends on the beauty and harmony of the object perceived; in fiction, these qualities are equivalent to verisimilitude – what is deemed reasonably possible. The two key statements in the Canon of Toledo's discourse, mentioned above, are these:

What beauty can there be, or what proportion betwen parts and whole and vice-versa, in a book or fable where a lad of sixteen stabs a giant as big as a tower and splits him in two as if he were made of sugar paste?

(i, 565)

and

Fictitious fables must be wedded to the intelligence of their readers and be so written that, by making the impossible seem easy and prodigies seem plain, and by keeping the reader's spirit in suspense, they arouse wonderment, suspense, joy, and pleasure. . . and none of these things can be achieved by him who flees verisimilitude and imitation, in which literary perfection consists.   (*ibid.*)

From the second statement it is evident that Cervantes's notions of verisimilitude or imitation of nature are very different from notions of realism based, say, on the nineteenth-century novel (Riley 1962, chapter 5). He takes for granted that the writer of heroic romance – the genre to which he is referring – will aim at effects such as wonderment, suspense, and joy, and will depict things extraordinary yet possible, rather than the routine stuff of everyday experience. That saving phrase 'yet possible' marks a crucial distinction for Cervantes: all the difference between the idea of a lad of sixteen splitting a giant in half and the extra-ordinary coincidences of the Captive's story (*DQ* I, 39–42), which occur in a recognisably contemporary and historical world, *could* happen, and therefore merit the description *verdaderas* ('true', i.e. as if true). Thus, Cervantes's basic motive in attacking the romances is his sense that demolition must precede re-construction; as a professional writer of entertainment drawn to this general kind of fiction, he felt indignant about the massive pro-liferation of an inferior species of it which had perverted public taste and queered his own pitch.

At this point his motives for writing *Don Quixote* shade from the aesthetic into the personal, and reflect cultural and social influences other than those mentioned. What is known of his biography (McKendrick 1980) suggests that he may have been, by contrast with some famous literary contemporaries, a somewhat marginal and unfortunate figure. The grievances imputed to him have unduly if understandably influenced the interpretation of his attitude to the society around him. The son of a poor surgeon, he was born in 1547, finished his education at a humanist academy in Madrid (not a university), and suddenly left Spain for Italy in 1569. His probable involvement in a duel may explain this departure; it would also provide the motive for his insistent repudiation of revenge in his writings. By 1570, he had enlisted in the Spanish army in Italy. Now begins the heroic period recalled in the Captive's story; it includes his participation in the sea-battle of Lepanto (1571) and the five years of his captivity in Algiers. Ransomed in 1580, he returned to Spain, settled in Madrid, and began a moderately successful literary career as dramatist and author of a pastoral romance, *La Galatea* (1585). Then, in 1587, he quit literature for more humdrum and aggravating occupations, including that of tax-collector, which brought him a spell of imprisonment in 1597 for a shortfall in the revenues due to the Spanish Treasury. This was not due to his dishonesty, but to the bankruptcy of a Sevillian banker. *Don Quixote* was supposedly 'engendered' (*DQ* I, Prologue) in this three-month internment.

When, about 1600, he resumed his leisure and his pen, he must already have become aware of the enormous success of the New Comedy, led by Lope de Vega; this made the actor-managers reluctant to buy his plays. The New Comedy's formula was avowedly popular and unclassical: it drew on national traditions; it triumphally expressed the prevailing social ethos – patriotic, devout, obsessed with honour; it cultivated speed and variety of action, sensationalism, the mixing of genres. There now occurs a relative redirection of Cervantes's creative energies, from 'poetry' (including drama) to prose-fiction; to attribute it chiefly to the above-mentioned circumstances would be simplistic, yet they undoubtedly help to explain it. Though he acknowledged

Lope de Vega's supreme talent, he regarded some of his and his followers' success as due to unscrupulous pandering to vulgar taste. In *DQ* I, 48 he equates the New Comedy's violations of the classical rules with the aberrations of chivalric romances. Some of the polemical bite of Part I, and much of the witty malice of its prologue, issue from a general resentful sense of artistic standards cheapened, outlets blocked, and opportunities lost to luckier rivals.

After the enthusiastic reception of Part I, both in Spain and abroad, Cervantes mellowed. Until his death in 1616, he lived chiefly in Madrid. Towards the end, the patronage of the Archbishop of Toledo and the Count of Lemos somewhat alleviated his chronic poverty; he was now famous, and had achieved some social recognition. In a glorious Indian summer of creativity, which, if we include the composition of Part I, lasted from his early fifties to his sixty-ninth year, he completed the two Parts of *Don Quixote* (1605; 1615), his twelve *Exemplary Novellas* (1613), the poem *Voyage to Parnassus* (1614), a collection of comedies and farces (1615), and *Persiles* (posthumously published, 1617), not to mention work unpublished or unfinished. Two factors help to explain this prodigious output. First, the success of *Don Quixote* Part I primed the pump of reader demand. Secondly, in Madrid Cervantes was surrounded by writers of talent or genius: rivalry, emulation, and intimacy with their writings primed *his* pump. In particular, the climate of early seventeenth-century Spain – golden zenith of its Golden Age – was propitious for the writing of works in a satiric vein: Quevedo's *Sueños* or visions of hell; Góngora's and Quevedo's humorous poetry; the picaresque; *Don Quixote*; some of Cervantes's short stories. Historical reasons help to explain this.

The Spain of Philip II (1556–98), despite setbacks, was still a confident nation, proud of its leadership of Catholic Christendom. The Spain of Philip III, that of Cervantes's Indian summer, was more passive and introspective. It had to cope with the financial exhaustion to which Philip II had brought it; hence it curbed military adventures abroad. The court, based in Madrid from 1606, belied this retrenchment and indulged in conspicuous extravagance. Powerful court-favourites ran the country for the colourless monarch, and their influence reflected the ascendancy and wealth of the aristocracy, which paralleled those of the Church, and contrasted with the poverty of the rest of the nation. Madrid became a centre of leisure, opportunity, and smart residence; swarms of people came to it from the impoverished provinces to seek preferment at court or service in noble households. Art – theatre, lyric poetry, painting, fiction – flourished; the Inquisition's censorship may have checked intellectual enquiry, yet it did not curb creativity. By its policy of enforced religious unity, Spain avoided the religious conflicts that shook its European neighbours. At the same time, it lost some of the accompanying intellectual ferment. It also experienced a different kind of internal dissension, originating from the socially stigmatised, hence disaffected descendants of converted Jews and Moors. The latter, the *moriscos*, were expelled from Spain between 1609 and 1614 (see *DQ* II, 54). This was a society hyperconscious of honour, status, and caste. The gentry pursued a life of dignified idleness; those lower down the social pyramid sought unscrupulously to scramble up. Widespread religious fervour, propagated by the Catholic Counter-Reformation, was matched by the dissolution and violence of *mores*. The comic writers of the age gleefully catalogue and ridicule the teeming human fauna around them and, not infrequently, each other. Quevedo, from his Stoic, aristocratic, and conservative viewpoint, was cynically convinced of living in a society corrupted by money and the loss of ancestral moral fibre and sense of hierarchy; *desengaño*, disenchantment with worldly vanity, is his insistent theme.

Don Quixote, with its literary theme, part-idealised rural settings, and holiday atmosphere, seems at first to say little about all this. On closer inspection it proves to say much by implication: e.g. in its portrayal of a counterfeit *caballero* or the life of pleasure-seeking aristocrats. Yet Cervantes's forte as a comic writer consists in showing the warts on man's private rather than his public face and perceiving a universal representativeness in them.

The social (as distinct from literary) satire in *Don Quixote* is indirect and sublimated in this comic vision. While Cervantes offers a grandly sweeping representation of his society and epoch, its tone is harmonious, mellow, and picturesque, rather than caustic. One reason for this is that his novel, though an attack on heroic literature, conserves a partly heroic or romantic tone. Another is its creator's conception of the comic.

The prologues to Cervantes's works, similar in tone to Horace's *Satires*, let the reader into his intimacy. They show him affably conversing with friends, including the reader in this category; the tone is self-deprecating, anecdotal, disarming, jocular. The prologue to *Don Quixote* Part I portrays him, unforgettably, in a dithering quandary, cheek on hand, elbow on desk, not knowing how to proceed until rescued by his facetious counsellor; in the prologue to Part II, similarly bantering, he sends the reader off as an emissary to Avellaneda – the man who, under this pseudonym, published a continuation of Part I a year before the publication of Cervantes's Part II – with a couple of jokes about madmen and dogs, the second one cheerfully vulgar. Both have disparaging implications about his rival's leaden wit. Prefatory matters are not extraneous to *Don Quixote* since much of it, notably Part II, might be considered a continuation of its prologues, and since its humour is stamped with authorial personality. The moving prologue to *Persiles*, written when Cervantes was on his death-bed, contains his farewell to life, and specifically to laughter and friends. His priorities are revealing. When, in Chapter 4 of *Viaje del Parnaso*, he sums up his achievement in *Don Quixote*, he claims: 'I have given a means of diversion to the melancholy and downcast spirit in any time or season.' Thus, he shares the Renaissance's belief in laughter's therapeutic powers, attested by Rabelais's *Gargantua* and *Pantagruel*, Erasmus's *Praise of Folly*, Burton's *The Anatomy of Melancholy*, and diverges from the aggressive coarseness of Spanish humour of the age – perhaps a safety-value for its sense of decorum. Hence the ethos of *Don Quixote* is marked by conviviality, a festival spirit, levelling irony, and a kind of innocence. This is a world, like that of Boccaccio's *Decameron*, where care has been banished in a mood of civilised, communal fun. If *Don Quixote* attacks chivalric romances with such vigorous merriment, this is because they represent human folly in an impersonal form: the extravagances of a now somewhat outworn genre. Since Cervantes's emphasis falls on 'merriment' rather than 'attacks', he would probably have conceived of it as comedy rather than as satire.

The basic burlesque formula

Though Cervantes does not classify his novel generically, he implies that it has a basically parodic or satiric aim by playing variants on the idea of demolishing chivalric romances: e.g. 'inveighing against', 'undoing the authority and sway', 'knocking down the ill-founded machine' (Prologue to Part I). 'Demolition' is certainly *le mot juste* for the battering-ram comedy of the hero's adventures in Part I.

The novel's opening shows him imaginatively creating for himself, out of his unpromising circumstances, a suitable title, a steed, armour, a mistress, and – in Chapter 7 – a squire. This Edenic process of naming is revealing: an unworthy word-stem is grotesquely made to bear an idealistic flower. 'Quijote' is the name of a thigh-piece of a suit of armour; it rhymes with heroic 'Lanzarote' (Lancelot) and plays on the hero's surname, eventually said to be 'Quijano' Yet the suffix '-ote' is pejorative in Spanish; and the linking of the name with the province (*cf.* Amadís de Gaula) has a comically homely effect. Dulcinea is a treacly enhancement of the plain Jane rusticity of Aldonza, derived from 'dulce' (sweet). The Spanish proverb says: 'If you haven't a wench, Aldonza will do.' The Aldonza in question is a country lass whom Don Quixote had once fancied. The name 'Rocinante' is an attempt to bestow dignity on the bony nag in Don Quixote's stable: i.e., 'rocín (nag), 'antes' (before), but now a steed. Only the squire's name is unchanged. 'Sancho' is proverbially rustic; Panza means belly; and the character of the man is basically that of the clowns of sixteenth-century comedy: lazy, greedy, cheeky, loquacious, cowardly, ignorant, and above all, nitwitted.

The first two chapters are intended to clarify the hero's psychology, assumed to be extraordinary, by showing his symmetrical repetition of seminal habits of thought. The first of these habits is his assumption that imitating or going through the motions or imaginatively ascribing is the same as being or doing or perceiving; as Sancho observes (II, 10), he tends imaginatively to ascribe white to black. The ramifications of this motive are brilliantly developed. His aim is to *be* a hero of chivalric romance, that is, of a chivalric *history*, since the romances, for him, are true histories (*DQ* I, 1). Accordingly, he has only to imitate them for all that happens in them to happen to him. Since, as he supposes, this fictional world is real, so are its personages; hence, he claims almost to have seen Amadís with his own eyes, and on the strength of that, offers a precise description (*DQ* II, 1). Implicitly believing other people's fictions, he logically believes his own; so he is able simultaneously to admit that Dulcinea is an idealised figment and to request Sancho to deliver a love-letter to her (I, 25). Arguing the historical truth of chivalry books with the judicious Canon of Toledo (I, 49), he disconcerts his adversary with his crazily erudite jumbling of fact and legend, putting on the same level a historic tourney of 1434, the love of Tristan and Isolde, the peg with which Pierre of Provence guided his wooden horse through the air, and so on. During the performance of Master Peter's puppet-show he confuses theatre with reality, attacking the paste-board figures with his sword (II, 26). His motivation, madly different from sane idealism, is reader's make-believe exaggerated to the point where 'willing suspension of disbelief' has turned to total abandonment.

Chapter 2 illustrates a motive linked to the one mentioned above: 'all that he thought, saw or imagined seemed to him to be done or happen as he had read' (i, 82). This carries a rider, not stated but strongly implied: 'especially if the thing perceived offered a suitable stimulus to his expectant fantasy'. There is, clearly, a potential contradiction between this rider and seeing black as white. In this chapter the contradiction is stark and unresolved. Cervantes relates that at dusk the hero saw an inn which triggered the perception of a castle with is four towers, spires of gleaming silver, drawbridge, and deep moat. The two prostitutes at the door, travelling to Seville with some mule drovers, seemed to him like beautiful damsels or gracious ladies taking solace at the castle gate. The innkeeper offers *truchuela* for supper, meaning salt cod, and is misunderstood to mean little trout: food fit for a knight. Clinching proof is provided during the repast by a swine castrator's reed whistle, 'as a result of which he was quite convinced that he was in some famous castle, that he was being served to the accompaniment of music, that the cod was trout, the bread pure white, the prostitutes ladies, and that the innkeeper was the chatelain. And so he considered his resolve and sally well worth while' (i, 87). The mental process is madly circular. A predisposition to see black as white is accompanied by a need for reassurance that the world out there really is white and he is the fitting centre of it. This form of active self-delusion is related to his impulse to evade inconvenient evidence, perceptible in his reluctance to test the makeshift helmet a second time (I, 1).

The black-and-white opposition implies a split perspective on events, one sane, the other deluded. In the early chapters we are encouraged to adopt the first in a spirit of sardonic detachment from the second. The narrator's voice, judgements, and sarcastic wit predominate and coincide with the attitudes of the hero's chief interlocutors. For example, Cervantes's flat judgement about 'that counterfeit figure bearing such ill-assorted arms' is echoed in the prostitutes' titters (I, 2). By implication, we are included in that knot of spectators gazing in astonishment at the self-absorbed figure in the moonlight as he keeps vigil over his armour (I, 3). The conception of the hero is powerfully suggestive, but external and limited. His discourse is stiffly imitative, bristling with chivalric literature's archaisms and trite formulae and, notably in Chapter 5, with quotations that imply his identification with other literary heroes. There is little effective communication between him and others, little dialogue and much misunderstanding.

This external viewpoint is heavily influenced by some traditional comic stereotypes. In Italian and Spanish lore, inns and innkeepers were respectively renowned as places of ludicrous mishap and purveyors of ribald badinage, bread as black as the linen, the proverbial cat masquerading as hare (Joly 1982). In Chapter 3, the innkeeper offers an account of his youthful 'chivalric' exploits in the red light districts and rough docks and fisheries of Spain – a sort of delinquent grand tour that Cervantes typically associates with the figure of the *pícaro*. It seems to me hardly a coincidence that near the start of the famous picaresque novel *Guzmán de Alfarache* (Part I, 1599), a squalid inn is treated as the young *pícaro's* theatre of initiation in human perfidy. That is, it seems likely that Cervantes took the idea from Mateo Alemán, though the uncertainty surrounding the date and circumstances of composition of the early chapters of *Don Quixote* Part I makes one unable to be positive about this. Certainly the second inn visited by Don Quixote (I, 16), very similar in its wretched discomforts to the first, has a picaresque genealogy. Thus the launching of the hero's career is irredeemably base. Since the outer symbols of a knight's honour and vocation – his steed, armour, and dubbing – traditionally had an aura of sacrosanct dignity, the circumstances in which Don Quixote receives the order of chivalry utterly disqualify him. His 'patron', the innkeeper, is a mischievous rascal; quasi-liturgical gibberish is read out from the book of fodder accounts; a prostitute girds on the sword. Prior to that Don Quixote receives ironic precepts of chivalry from his patron in the form of advice about equipment: a well-stuffed purse, a change of shirts, a first-aid bag, saddle-bags, and a squire. This lecture, humming with leitmotifs that await future development, exudes something like the cynically materialistic philosophy of Spain's first *pícaro*, Lazarillo de Tormes, and his blind mentor.

In a general way, *Don Quixote's* initial form resembles many *novelas* (including Cervantes's own) and chapters of picaresque

novels which depict a character's extraordinary aberration prior
to relating the *burlas* – practical jokes, and by extension, mishaps
or deceptions – which befall him in consequence of it. *Burlas*
form the backbone of incident in the age's comic literature. Don
Quixote's gallantries to women of easy virtue in the early chapters
of Part I (also in I, 16 and 43) bring to mind the stories by Boccaccio and Bandello in which deluded lovers are tricked into making
love to repulsive sluts as though they were beautiful ladies. The
dubbing scene in I, 3 conforms to the type of joke played by
Boccaccio's Bruno and Buffalmacco on simple Calandrino (e.g.
Decameron VIII, 3). Its cast consists of a dupe, a mischievous
trickster, his accomplices and a knowing audience; the plot shows
how the dupe is tricked with a cock-and-bull story into undertak-
ing a ludicrous enterprise. The premise of such tales is that though
the mischief-maker stoops beneath the reader's sense of propriety, he articulates his sense of fun. The set-piece *burlas* of *Don
Quixote*, including the elaborate series in the Duke's palace (II,
30 ff.), conform to this model. Many of the adventures at inns or
by the roadside involve stereotyped *burlas* of a simpler kind: e.g.
the blanketing of Sancho (I, 17), the pelting with stones that
master and squire suffer from the galley-slaves (I, 22).

Thus, at the outset, Cervantes establishes a stratum of burlesque comedy which is basic to the sequel. He does not achieve
it by imitation of other works of parody but by a sort of fusion of
genres. He encases an imaginary chivalric romance, brought alive
by the hero's behaviour, in a frame derived from the sources just
mentioned. Delusions of grandeur are pitted against base reality,
and from that friction parody results.

The black-and-white opposition soon undergoes refinement.
This process is attributable to the following factors: Cervantes's
tendency, after the early chapters, quietly to omit explanations
about the hero's motives, assuming them to be already intelligible; his cultivation of objectivity, verisimilitude, and an empathetic, quasi-heroic type of parody; his conception of 'common
nature'; his indulgently humourous predilection for merry
imbroglios and a dialogue rich in 'character' where folly, instead

of being cleverly put in its place, artlessly projects itself and clashes with its own kind; his variation of the main theme with 'episodes' – e.g. romantic interludes – which have a harmonic affinity with the hero's delusion and provide a frame, more potential than actual in Part I, for the intervals of lucidity in his madness. With these developments the initially judicial, sardonic, and explanatory manner becomes urbanely light, playful, and non-committal. The developments are integral to the evolutionary, experimental tendency of the first two internal divisions – which Cervantes calls 'parts' – of Part I. Indeed, *Don Quixote* never really sheds its evolutionary habit. Modern criticism has tended to treat this process of change, however its nature and stages are defined, as involving a transformation of the novel's premises. Thus, the narrator becomes emotionally identified with the hero (Menéndez Pidal 1948), or adopts an increasingly relativistic viewpoint on his affairs (Riley 1986, chapter 13). I see the novel's basic rudiments as fixed at the start of internal 'part' three (I, 15); these, with the black-and-white opposition, persist in the later modifications.

The narrator's persona

Who narrates *Don Quixote*? Within the terms of Cervantes's story, there is an official and an implied answer. Officially, the narrator is the Moor Cide Hamete Benegeli (the 'first author'), whose chronicle is translated by another Moor and edited by Cervantes (the 'second author'); implicitly, as the reader perfectly well knows, the narrator is Cervantes himself, whose 'I' is powerfully projected by the novel's famous first sentence: 'In a place in La Mancha, whose name I do not choose to recall. . .'. The official pretence parodies one that recurs in chivalric romances and has a long medieval ancestry; it goes back to Archbishop Turpin's 'chronicle' of the exploits of Charlemagne's paladins. Authors of medieval prose romances, and their Spanish successors, wanted to invest fiction with something like the solemn authority of reliably attested history; Cervantes's invention of Benengeli aims largely to expose and debunk that ambiguous and (for the vulgar) misleading impression. There is a splendid spoof of the venerable pretence in the prologue to Folengo's *Le Maccharonee* (1521), where the 'editor' tells how he and some herbalist friends found the Macaronic corpus of Merlin Coccaio, together with the eleven tombs of the principals in *Baldus*, in a cavern in Armenia. Folengo's book was known to Rabelais, and also, independently, to Cervantes, who imitates it in Part I's conclusion. Benengeli is introduced with a splendid flourish in Part I, Chapter 9, where Cervantes recounts how he discovered the Moor's manuscript in a street-bazaar in Toledo. The anecdote has the particularised, enthusiastic tone of a diligent researcher's account of a tremendous find: casual interception of a transaction between a silk-merchant and a boy selling papers to him; search for an interpreter to translate a folder of papers in Arabic script; excited curiosity aroused by the marginal note: 'This Dulcinea del Toboso . . . is reputed to have had the best hand for salting pork amongst all the women of La Mancha' (i, 143); excited confirmation of source B's authenticity by comparison of its version of the battle with the Basque – illustrated for good measure – with that in source A (the unspecified 'autor' whose information had maddeningly run out at the battle's most interesting moment). Yet mention of Benengeli thereafter in Part I is infrequent; it dries up after Chapter 27. The preponderance of romantic episodes in the second half of Part I helps to explain this silence. Yet, in a general way, the announcement of his existence marks an important stage in the transformation of the narrator's manner from causticity to playful detachment; another stage is the introduction of Sancho, with its incentive to self-effacement.

In Part II, the seed planted early in Part I flourishes prodigiously. Why? Because Cervantes has woven into his story the facts of Part I's publication and of its immense popularity. Though not foreseen in Part I, this outcome is quite compatible with its premise: that it is a laudatory chronicle of the exploits of a Manchegan knight living in modern times (I, 9). So, very early in Part II, master and squire learn of the existence of 'Benengeli's chronicle'; other characters know them as the celebrities recorded in it, and their behaviour is conditioned by the knowledge. When, from Chapter 59, Cervantes begins to allude to Avellaneda's continuation of Part I, he proudly differentiates between Benengeli's authentic chronicle and the spurious one. Contrary to what has been claimed (e.g. by Thomas Mann 1969), there is no dissolution of the fictional frame in all this. When the two heroes meet their readership, they do so, not as heroes of a novel but as subjects of a biography, logically capable of discussing with other people the fairness or otherwise of their portrayal in it and the worthlessness of the rival biography which has blackened their characters and recorded the doings of fantastic, inferior surrogates. Even a sly-boots like Sansón Carrasco is oblivious to his irony, a wink privately directed by the author to the reader above his characters' heads. These are not 'the trick mirrors and false bottoms of artistic illusion' (Mann, p. 55); in this novel, what you see is what you get. For this reason, Cervantes's sophisticated whimsy is also naive – naive in its literalness and celebratory purpose. That Part II is not consequently suffused with insufferable smugness is due to the fact that the historical world is bent to the laws of the fictitious one. Thus, we are essentially concerned with Cervantes's book and Avellaneda's as refracted by Quixote's and Sancho's eccentric vision of things and self-image. The 'authors' are treated as the characters' puppets – attendant on their deeds, butts of their criticism (II, 3 and 7) – rather than vice versa. Cervantes's humorous self-disparagement in all this is quite disarming.

That Benengeli's book is both true and laudatory is obviously a preposterous spoof by Cervantes, who signals this with gay blatancy. Benengeli is a deformation of the Arabic for 'aubergine-like'; a popular expression linking Toledans to aubergines explains this 'etymology'. As a *morisco*, member of a despised ethnic minority, our 'first author' has most unsuitable credentials for hymning a Spanish hero, and indeed, even for qualifying as a historian. For how can a member of a race of liars possibly be veridical? Cervantes acknowledges the contradiction, accusing

Benengeli of 'falling short' of the truth by not praising the hero as he deserves (I,9). Here he lets the cat out of the bag, alluding to the novel's fictitiousness and its comicality. Alternatively, he achieves the same result by emphasising Benengeli's punctiliousness, or regretting its failures, when the facts in question are plainly trivial or absurd: such as the question whether the two heroes slept between ilexes or cork-trees (II, 60). Since the novel revolves around its hero, the pretence of historicity and the narrative manner in general are geared to his assumptions. Matching his premise that a record of his deeds must be 'grandílocua, alta, insigne, magnífica y verdadera' (II, 3; ii, 58), they mimic the personae and flourishes of the epic narrator and the historian's scrupulous quibbles about the reliability of evidence. Yet they do so in a flippantly subversive way. The very genesis of Benengeli is inspired by Don Quixote's imagination of the sage who, in a future chronicle of his deeds, will find suitably florid words to extol his early morning ride across the plain of Montiel (I, 2). A few chapters later, Cervantes gives body to this fantasy. The relation of the great find is preceded by a passage in which Cervantes expresses perplexity that so worthy a knight should have lacked what all others had: 'one or two sage enchanters, made to measure, who not only wrote down his deeds, but would depict his most insignificant thoughts and childish follies' (I, 9; i, 140). The words sum up Benengeli's intimate and debunking relation to Don Quixote: Boswell to his Johnson, with an eye firmly fixed on the absurdly humdrum.

Modern Cervantine criticism, with its insistence on a variety of narrative viewpoints, versions, or masks tends to obscure these motives by treating them as subordinate to others of a suspiciously twentieth-century character: 'How does art give an effect of truth-to-life in an age deeply conscious of mind's subjectivity?' Such interpretations imply that in some significant sense the personae and versions of Benengeli and his editor are credibly distinct. The deliberate vagueness, absurdity, and inconsistency of the fictitious authorship make it impossible to conceive of Benengeli other than as a comic fantasm conjured up by the editor's references and indistinguishable from him. As soon as we try to give substance to the fantasm it dissolves. Now it is suggested that the chronicle is incredibly up-to-date (II, 2–3), now old parchments in Gothic script are invoked (I, 52), now it is flippantly implied that facts have been ascertained by magical telepathy (II, 2 and *cf.* I, 19), now by more orthodox means: personal testimony, hearsay, even another history (II, 4 and 24). Hydra-like, Benengeli's text multiplies. The translator speaks of apocryphal additions to it (II, 5), and the editor mesmerisingly alludes to folk-traditions of what Benengeli wrote in a primitive version, but suppressed from the definitive one (II, 12). To treat all this as evidence of Benengeli's 'unreliability' solemnly misses the point; this is a comic novel; the taking of certain liberties with consistency is part of the fun. The jest has a serious purpose only in a figurative dimension, as Riley pointed out (1962, p. 171): it refers to the book's plausibility, as contrasted with the impossibility of chivalry books (II, 16).

If we wish to make accusations of unreliability, we should look to the editor, who so cavalierly exercises his prerogative. Who, for example, is responsible for the playful invocation to Apollo at the beginning of II, 45:

Oh perpetual discoverer of the Antipodes, torch of the world, eye of the sky, sweet swayer of water canteens, Timbrio here, Phoebus there, bowman hither, doctor thither, father of poetry, inventor of music, you who always rise, and though it appears so, never set! To you, I say, oh sun, with whose help man engenders man, grant me your aid. (ii, 375)

The mighty task in question is the narration of Sancho's governorship. The speaker cannot be Benengeli, whose interventions are habitually identified. In that case, what business has the editor of a *history* to appeal to the god of *poetry* for inspiration? The nonchalant disregard for consistency is typical. If we try to distinguish this as 'editorial comment' from 'the narrative proper' we face difficulties: this slippage from editorial impersonality to subjectivity is frequent in the novel; also, the passage's urbane burlesque of humanistic erudition is continuous with the humorous grace-notes which pervade the narrative discourse – parodies of the hero's turns of phrase, mock hyperboles and maxims, epithets, word-plays of various species, intensifying analogies (Rosenblat 1971). Thus, the question of who narrates *Don Quixote* converts into one about how it is narrated. This tone may be described as sustained jocular whimsy which, by its blend of fulsome mock-gravity and familiar irreverence, makes transparent its real origin and the innocent absurdity of its subject-matter. It is a highly *self*-conscious manner. At the novel's conclusion, Cervantes emphasises his indivisibility from Benengeli: 'Such was the end of the ingenious *hidalgo* of La Mancha, whose place of origin Cide Hamete did not choose to specify.' This echoes the novel's self-assertive opening. Also, Benengeli's valediction to his quill, a parody of the shepherd's to his flute in Virgil's eighth eclogue, echoes Cervantes's claims of creative fatherhood and copyright in the prologues to *Don Quixote*. The very manner of Benengeli's introduction in I, 9, where Cervantes portrays himself in a frustrated quandary until rescued by the Moor's manuscript, reminds us of his self-portrayal in the prologue to Part I. Benengeli is the clownish persona which Cervantes has assumed to tell his story; his personality, apparently effaced, is omni-present.

Empathetic parody; comic and satiric modes

Considered as a writer of comic fiction, Cervantes differs from his contemporaries and precursors in this principal respect: he approaches it with preconceptions derived from the practice of romantic fiction. In this, he tends to launch sequences of incident with mysterious and dramatic happenings which provoke the curiosity of witnesses – in effect, proxies for the reader within the fictional world. They observe the unravelling of these mysteries by hearing the strangers involved in them recount their tribulations; they note the connections between these testimonies and others; they witness the reunions and recognitions which undo the tangled knots. They way in which the affairs of Cardenio and

Dorotea are presented is a good example of this technique (I, 23–29 and 36); here, the principal witnesses are Don Quixote and the priest. The underlying purpose is to heighten the story's suspense, immediacy, and emotiveness for the reader and multiply the pleasurable wonder of its peripeties.

The implementation of this quasi-theatrical form of narrative in *Don Quixote* has major consequences. It partly explains Cervantes's tendency to curb his own interventions and to present scenes or conversations as the witnesses or participants see or hear them. The graphic energy of his descriptions is largely due to this, they are almost rhetorically addressed to the interested bystander. When we discover that buried, half-rotten suitcase in the *sierra* – the first clue leading to Cardenio – we scour every nook and cranny of it through Sancho's covetous eyes (I, 23). When we see Don Quixote doing battle with the wine-skins, clad in red greasy nightcap and scanty nightshirt, and displaying long hairy dirty legs, we register these details from the viewpoint of Dorotea – Velázquez-like observer in the open doorway – who takes one look and modestly averts her gaze (I, 35). The scene's comicality for us is enhanced by its effect on her. Despite its hilarity, it is related with factual sobriety, motivated by the concern to explain the prodigy plausibly, provoke wonder as well as laughter, and, in general, stick to 'the facts' and cut out frills. These aims are stated or clearly implied in the comments on the narrative of Master Peter's apprentice (II, 26), the prologue to Part I, and elsewhere. They are responsible for Cervantes's famous objectivity, which, it should be noted, is not neutrality. We may, temporarily, share Sancho's eyesight; we remain ironically detached from his greed.

This empathetic form of presentation generates an empathetic kind of parody, which has an internal relation to its object. Cervantes creates ambivalently harmonic affinities between the phenomena that herald each adventure and Don Quixote's predisposition, and this partly converts him from object into subject: whereas at first he is chiefly a butt of other people's wondering scrutiny, they soon acquire that status for him. The harmonic affinities are manifest in the adventure of the 'liberation' of Andrés (I, 4). Though somewhat vestigial in the adventures which immediately follow, they are still discernible there: for instance, the hero's joust with the windmills is provoked, as he implies, by their metonymic relationship to giants (I, 8). These affinities are fully established in the five famous adventures near the middle of Part I (sheep, funeral cortège, fulling mills, basin, galley slaves). Here, Don Quixote's misapprehensions appear naturally triggered by their cause. Since his ensuing enactment of a chivalric role is, with qualifications to be noted, stylish, informed, serious, and psychologically credible, we are encouraged to share his imaginative self-immersion in his chivalric world, just as we share Sancho's eyesight (but not greed) in the incident mentioned.

The description of the setting in which master and squire find themselves in Part I, Chapter 20 is eerily suggestive: a wood of tall trees with leaves rustling in the wind; a dark night; and from somewhere nearby, a mighty crash of water accompanied by a sinister pounding and creaking of chains. Don Quixote 'with his intrepid heart, leapt on Rocinante, and, clasping his shield, tilted his lance and' launched into a pompously self-glorifying speech. Cervantes's empathetic method is well illustrated by the words just quoted; the hero's actions are painted just as he would wish. Reciprocally, in the central passage of the speech, the hero echoes the very motifs of his creator's scene-setting:

Bien notas, escudero fiel y legal, las tinieblas desta noche, su estraño silencio, el sordo y confuso estruendo destos árboles, el temeroso ruido de aquella agua en cuya busca venimos, que parece que se despeña y derrumba desde los altos montes de la Luna, y aquel incesable golpear que nos hiere y lastima los oídos; las cuales cosas, todas juntas y cada una por sí, son bastantes a infundir miedo, temor y espanto en el pecho del mesmo Marte. (i, 238)

Well do you mark, good and faithful squire, the darkness of this night, its strange silence, the muffled and confused din of these trees, the fearful roar of that water in search of which we come, apparently precipitating itself and crashing down from the high mountains of the Moon, and that incessant pounding which wounds and afflicts our ears; all of which, separately and together, is sufficient to instil fear, dread and horror in Mars himself.

From these circumstances Don Quixote will infer his dauntless courage, merely fired by what would have made Mars quake. Apparently he and Cervantes speak in unison. The effect is strengthened by the speech's Ciceronian grandeur. Examples of it, in the Spanish quotation, are the artful internal rhymes split and lengthened by double consonants (e.g. 'estruendo'/'silencio'), the balanced synonyms and grammatical structures giving an effect of musical phrasing, impressive amplification of circumstances, the scansion of members in a proportionately augmenting sequence. Nonetheless, the speech is fissured by absurd ironies. The legal formula 'escudero fiel y legal' and the analogies with Mars and the Ethiopian origins of the Nile sustain a tone of high pomposity. The speech's messianic opening, marked with the triumphant anaphora of 'yo nací. . .yo soy. . .yo soy' ('I was born. . .I am. . .I am. . .') and announcing Don Quixote's destiny to revive the golden age of chivalry in an age of iron and eclipse all the famous heroes of the past, has an authentically chivalric ring. Similar portentous forecasts are frequently made in chivalry books, yet with one important difference: they are made by the narrator, the enchanter who presides over the hero's destiny, *not* by the hero himself. Amadís, paragon of modesty, would have cringed at such bombast, which flouts Don Quixote's own precept: 'self-praise is demeaning' (I, 16). This part of the speech carries forward his eccentric rationale of the history of knight-errantry and his place in it (*cf*. I, 5, 11 and 13) – eccentric, because it treats the myth of the Golden Age and the legends of the Round Table as historical fact. Don Quixote's situation is freely modelled on the build-up to Amadís's battle with a monster in *Amadís de Gaula*, Chapter 73. As Amadís's squire does on that occasion, Sancho bursts into tears on hearing his master's foolhardy resolve and begs him to desist. The plea, unlike Gandalín's reaction, reveals Sancho's concern for his own skin; it is a travesty of the rhetoric of entreaty by virtue of the diversity, baseness, and spuriousness of the arguments: e.g. Nobody will be the wiser if we take another road; I shall die if you leave me here; I left wife and children to better my lot and now you do *this* to me.

Here begins the long process of flattening that heroic fanfare – the very purpose for which Cervantes gave it such specious elevation. It continues with Sancho's sly trick of hobbling Rocinante, his artlessly meandering and banal shaggy dog story, his contorted efforts to rid himself of his fear-induced burden without leaving his master's side, above all, by the discovery of the cause of the din on the following morning. Thus, Cervantes's initial empathy is an ironist's tactic: an inflation of the balloon prior to its puncture. this is apparent in the deliberate echoing of the fanfare when anti-climax is imminent and when it arrives. While Sancho's delaying tactics deliciously slacken the knot of suspense, they remind us that it remains to be unravelled. Cervantes tightens it at the eleventh hour by his marvellous description of Don Quixote's and Sancho's approach to the sound. It comically pictures their apprehension; thus, Sancho, not daring to leave his master's side, stretches his neck and peers through Rocinante's legs. Also, it reveals what they successively saw with tantalising gradualness: the chestnut trees; a meadow below high rocks from which a cataract tumbles; some derelict shacks. Then, after another hundred paces, round a bend, 'there, patent and exposed to view was the very unmistakable cause of that horrendous and dreadful din, which had kept them in such fearful suspense all night. It was, if it doesn't irritate and upset you, reader, six fulling-mill paddles, which caused the din by their alternate blows' (i, 248). This is a nice example of the humorous gracenotes mentioned previously. That wink of complicity at the reader, implying playful apology for having promised so much and delivered so little, is characteristic. Here, at the very moment of revelation, Cervantes repeats his anti-climactic delaying tactics, and echoes, in a tone of mock-awe, the terms of that eery scene-setting. Empathy and irony are inseparable.

The anti-climactic structure of this adventure is typical of Part I and has an evidently exemplary effect. Yet such exemplariness, appropriate to satire, is somewhat softened and qualified by the novel's comic ethos. I take 'comic' as referring to a literary mode which, insofar as it can be distinguished from satire, is less censorious than it and more concerned with operating the laughter-provoking mechanisms and situations that Bergson (1913) identifies in *Le Rire*: levelling (e.g. cardinal revealed as sot), inversion (e.g. prisoner rebukes judge), snowballing, repetition. With *Don Quixote* in mind, we can add some more categories to the list: 'standing on the evidence and failing to see it', 'proving nonsense true', 'hoist with own petard', 'the tables turned', 'Sod's law'. These and other situational ironies, like the novel's morals, are encapsulated in its proverbs. Bergson, who takes Cervantes's hero as a prime example of his theory of the mechanical nature of comic behaviour, derives most of his evidence from comic theatre; and this is an important source of inspiration for Cervantes too. In some adventures the balance tilts towards caustic exemplariness, in others towards the comic. I consider examples of both types in order to bring to light the novel's lessons and tone.

The hero's first adventure as an armed knight (I, 4) is initially presented with deliberate emotiveness and echoes of the felonies of chivalric romance: in response to piteous cries, he rides into a wood and sees, tied to a tree, a young boy being lashed with a belt by a burly man. His hectoring challenge to this 'knight' elicits a meek explanation of the rights and wrongs of the affair – rather different from the black and white picture that Don Quixote forms. The peasant claims that he is beating his shepherd-boy for negligence; the boy alleges that the beating is just a cloak for his master's reluctance to pay wages. The rate at which Andrés loses sheep – one a day – is as impressive as the wage-arrears – nine months at seven *reales* monthly. Juan Haldudo accepts the claim, and even Don Quixote's faulty computation, but argues that the price of two blood-lettings and of leather for three pairs of shoes must be discounted from the total. Don Quixote wittily retorts

that the boy's tanned hide and drawn blood cancel the discount.
He appears in command of the situation; yet it is evident that his
chivalric attitudes to the affair have become comically entangled
in the humdrum practicalities of a job dispute in which neither
side is blameless. The homely details about shoe-leather and
bleedings typify the distinctive quality of 'realism' in *Don Quixote*; they, rather than innkeepers 'more thieving than Cacchus'
(I, 2), represent the common nature that the hero ignores.

Now the balance of advantage shifts, and the shift is nicely
captured by the dialogue, which characterises the peasant's evas-
iveness and mockery (clearly, he doubts his adversary's sanity),
the boy's alarm at the prospect of being left alone with his tormen-
tor, and his champion's rash confidence in the peasant's promise
to pay the debt. Don Quixote declares: 'He will do no such thing.
My mere command is enough to ensure his respect; and provided
that he swears to pay by the order of knighthood that he has
received, I will let him go free and guarantee the payment' (i,
97). The superb arrogance of this declaration makes it stick in
our minds when it is refuted by the outcome. It illustrates a
method much favoured by satirists: to caricature their target as
a madly inflexible, circular, casuistical system of rules: e.g.
Catch-22, Pangloss's systematic optimism, the army of the Good
Soldier Švejk. Soon Don Quixote rides off. Having been humili-
ated before his servant, the peasant naturally thirsts for revenge,
but first he savours his moment by unctuously inviting Andrés to
come so that he may be 'paid' what he is 'owed'. The description
of how he is re-tied to the tree and thrashed till left for dead is
effectively laconic. *Quod erat demonstrandum*.

The irony of events has a classic force, by virtue of its emotive
air of violent injustice and of the stark, well-disguised contrast
between build-up and anti-climax, hubris and failure. We are
reminded of cynically instructive precursors: Aesop's fables
about the folly of trusting the fair words of rogues, Spanish folklore about peasant untrustworthiness, the *pícaro's* initiations in
human perfidy. The comeuppances of poor Lázaro de Tormes at
the hands of his masters are surely present in Cervantes's mind.

He has added caustic force to these traditional lessons. Whereas the fledgling *pícaro* is the direct victim of his own ingenuousness, the chief dupe in this case is the would-be champion, unaware of having compounded the injury of the intended beneficiary. There is Voltairean savagery in this. Cervantes marks it with his sardonic 'Thus did the valorous Don Quixote undo the offence', but otherwise makes no comment. This detachment is characteristic, yet it should not be confused with inscrutability. Andrés, on his re-appearance in I, 31, heaps reproaches on his self-imagined deliverer and offers conjectures as to what would have happened had he not intervened. After a few more blows, Juan Haldudo, his rage spent, would have untied his servant and paid him. The moral of the affair, as Cervantes sees it, is clear. Human nature, left to its own devices, would have produced a rough justice commensurate with the claims and grievances of both parties. Treating its grey nuances as though they were black and white makes such equilibrium impossible. The lessons of this adventure are paradigmatic in *Don Quixote*: the folly of trying to drive out Nature with a pitchfork (Horace, *Epistles* I, x, 24), of meddling where one is not called, of judging by appearances.

The encounter between Don Quixote and the Knight of the Wood in early Part II (12–14) richly exemplifies the situations identified by Bergson. Besides chivalry books, it spoofs those frequent meetings in Cervantes's romantic fiction between character A and a mysterious B, whose woeful story reveals his vital relationship to A and culminates in dramatic recognition. The episode is long and humorously discursive; I focus only on its nub: the strange knight's mendacious claim to have defeated a certain Don Quijote de la Mancha and caused him to confess Dulcinea's inferiority to his own lady. Don Quixote, dissimulating his astonishment with aplomb, politely suggests that the stranger has been victim of an enchanter's hallucination, then, timing his self-introduction nicely, undertakes to make good his assertion on the field of honour. Obviously the stranger is a mischievous prankster playing cat-and-mouse with the hero. But who is he and what's his game? Our discovery of the answers coincides with the realisation that the cat has fallen into the mouse-trap.

The description of the joust (II, 14) shows a brilliant sense of the indignities that menace mounted sportsmanship. The strange knight, seeing Don Quixote occupied in helping the terrified Sancho into a tree, sportingly checks his charge. Don Quixote, when ready, shows no such nice scruple but bears down on his adversary, frantically trying to spur his paralytic steed into motion. In this position of disadvantage he is humiliatingly unhorsed. And now, as Don Quixote unlaces the vanquished foe's helmet, comes the moment for which Cervantes has kept us waiting for nearly three chapters:

And he beheld. . .Who may say what he beheld without causing astonishment, wonder, and shock to the listeners? He beheld, relates the history, the very face, the very countenance, the very aspect, the very physiognomy, the very effigy, the very semblance of bachelor Sansón Carrasco.   (ii, 143)

Not 'he saw Sansón Carrasco'. Cervantes's mockingly saucer-eyed avoidance of the obvious mimics the hero's thoughts. For the fact that this looks exactly like Sansón Carrasco, the mischievous student from Don Quixote's village, in no way proves that it is he. It proves instead the power of enchanters; and Don Quixote excitedly summons Sancho to witness it. Sancho, nitwittedly accepting this assumption, suggests that the fantasm should be despatched with Don Quixote's lance. Sansón's squire Tomé Cecial, now without his disguise of a grotesque false nose, pleads with Don Quixote not to murder his good friend. Sancho, hearing his neighbour Tomé offer convincing proof of his own identity, does not know whom to believe. True anagnorisis should bring blinding recognition; this one merely brings blindness. The scene's cross-purpose confusions and dramatic ironies have an evident theatricality – no coincidence, since it is a re-play of a frustrated anagnorisis in one of Cervantes's comedies.

Sansón's clever ruse, designed to bring Don Quixote home and cure him, ridiculously backfires, 'because he didn't find nests where he thought to find birds' (II, 15; ii, 147). Here Cervantes plays with two Spanish proverbs about frustrated hopes. One says: 'There are no birds in yesteryear's nests', and the other: 'Some think to find bacon and don't even find poles [to hang it on]'. Don Quixote, euphoric after his victory, expects his foe to bring back news of the enchanted Dulcinea's condition (see p. 99), 'but he thought one thing and the knight of the Mirrors thought another' (ii, 146). Here Cervantes plays with another proverb: 'The bay horse thinks one thing, the groom another'. This verbal foolery and application of parallel proverbs to victor and vanquished show his gay neutrality. Obviously, Sansón is left looking the sillier: victim of Sod's Law, he has been hoist with his own petard, had the tables turned on him, and compounded confusion. In claiming to have defeated a knight exactly resembling Don Quixote, he has laid the basis for Don Quixote's conviction that his defeated foe, exactly resembling Sansón Carrasco, cannot possibly be he (II, 16). He also confirms Don Quixote's self-belief and his conviction about Dulcinea's enchantment, which, in argument with Sancho, he cites as clinching disproof of Sancho's doubts about the enchantment of Sansón and Tomé. Little does he realise that his argument is disastrously counter-productive, since Sancho himself faked Dulcinea's enchantment. Yet it puts his squire in an impossible dilemma. If he rebuts the argument by owning up to having lied about Dulcinea, he incriminates himself; if he keeps silent, he leaves his master with the last word. These brilliant spirals of situational irony show how the hero's delusion draws circular strength from its own premises, from *ad hoc* precedents, even from refutation. As in a dense system of poetic imagery, each piquant new convolution enriches the implications of its predecessors. It acquires a classic aura by its elegance, archetypal resonance, and psychological vividness. And what of the morals of the imbroglio that we have just considered? They concern the weaving of tangled webs, over-weaning presumption, and the self-protective nature of men's delusions.

Don Quixote Part I, by contrast with Part II, is dynamically rumbustious. The rhythm of the hero's adventures is hectic and upbeat, and flows, electrically charged, from him to his adversaries. In accordance with Renaissance psychology (Green 1970), Cervantes sees his madness as a psychophysical condition, aggravated by excitement and calmed by sleep, cooling draughts, distraction. In the adventures, it rises to hallucinatory fever pitch. In a sort of improvised chivalric ballet he sweeps his adversaries, willy-nilly dance-partners, through the steps leading to his expected fulfilment of the hero's role. They, disconcerted by the invasion of their private pursuits, either react with mischievous teasing or with hot-blooded panic, indignation, consternation. Their reluctance to dance to the required tune stokes Don Quixote's choler and provokes conflict: an exemplary travesty of what was intended. Common sense is proved right and he is proved wrong, usually in a physically humiliating way. Yet the lesson is wasted on him in the short term because his madness includes an india-rubber resilience and optimism, which allow him to multiply rare victories and shrug off defeats as accidental discomfitures caused by the rubs of fortune and envious enchanters.

The merrily narrated stonings, beatings, tumbles, and free-for-alls which typically round off the adventures epitomise Part I's rumbustiousness and its tendency to modulate from a satirically exemplary mode into a comic one. If Cervantes's mock-grave, empathetic method is a tactic of quiet irony, he offers plenty of advance signals – e.g. the above-mentioned hectic rhythm – of a farcical outcome in store. The scene of pandemonium at the inn (I, 45), if not literally the conclusion of Part I, is its true orchestral finale. A superb example of inversion, levelling, and snowballing, it is provoked in the same way as the fracas at the end of Cervantes's most famous farce, *The Marvellous Miniature Theatre*, and would have inevitably reminded contemporary readers of such dénouements:

The priest was shouting, the innkeeper's wife screaming, her daughter was in distress, Maritornes wept, Dorotea was in confusion, Luscinda in suspense, and Doña Clara in a swoon. The barber was pummelling Sancho and Sancho was pounding him; Don Luis, whom one of his servants had boldly seized by the arm so as to prevent him escaping, gave him a punch which bathed his teeth in blood; the magistrate defended him; Don Fernando had the body of a country policeman at his feet, trampling it up and down at will; the innkeeper raised his voice again requesting favour for the Holy Brotherhood, with the result that all the inn was sobs, cries, screams, confusion, fear, alarms, mishaps, stabs, punches, cudgellings, kicks, and spillage of blood.   (I, 45; i, 544)

By rhetorical standards the style is plain. It cuts out the ornaments of elegant prose, calls a spade a spade, and abruptly shifts from one hot-blooded act to another, showing brilliant virtuosity in the variation of terms. Hence the effect of crackling dynamism. Don Quixote's anarchic belligerence has mindlessly communicated itself to the whole throng. The barriers of social hierarchy and decorum are cast down. Poetic justice seems to have gone out of the window. Previously, Don Quixote's teeth were bathed in blood and his body was trampled (I, 16); now innocent third parties, including a law-officer, receive this treatment. Eventually, it is left to the Lord of Misrule himself to reduce chaos to order. Yet we discover that these denials and inversions of poetic justice are merely provisional. They take place under the benign aegis of Don Fernando and the priest, and are patched up by the liberality of the one and good offices of the other (beginning of Chapter 46). Inversion, levelling, and snowballing may nullify poetic justice temporarily; they only do so under licence and within the sphere of *burlas*. This holds true for the rest of *Don Quixote*.

Form of Part I; its episodes

Since its hero imitates the romances, so, at first, does *Don Quixote's* structure: pseudo-chronicle of a knight's wanderings in search of adventure. The incidents succeed each other like beads on a string: Cervantes profits by this loose, articulated assembly to vary the colour and nature of the beads. These, in Part I, are of three kinds: chivalric adventures interspersed by the hero's conversations with Sancho; critical discussions of the romances;

romantic interludes. These incidents are located in four kinds of setting, each with its appropriate atmosphere and associations: plain traversed by *camino real*, home, inns, wooded uplands. Adventures have a natural link with all scenarios save home; virtually the reverse is true of the critical discussions, which stand theoretically opposed to them. Two of the locations are ambivalent: Juan Palomeque's inn (I, 16-17 and 32-46) serves both as a degraded mock-castle and as a substitute for the enchanted castles of pastoral romance where love's maladies are cured. The *sierra* is both a theatre of romantic interludes and of chivalric adventures. The incidents of Part I are typically grouped in cycles, whose basis is the duration of a journey or a sojourn at an inn. The journey, in internal 'parts' two and three (Chapters 9–14 and 15–27), takes us from plain to wooded uplands, respectively, the typical scenarios of adventures and of interludes. The whole of Part I repeats this movement: outward journey to the *sierra* crammed with adventures; return via the inn with its cycle of interludes.

So, like a piece of jazz, Part I improvises within regulating patterns. Of its *ad hoc* mode of assembly there is plentiful evidence: signs of revision, omissions, happy afterthoughts, changes of plan (Stagg 1959). The most notorious of these is the affair of the theft and recovery of Sancho's ass (see *DQ* I, pp. 279–80, in Murillo's edition); both events go unmentioned in the first edition, with the result that the beast mysteriously disappears and reappears. One upshot of Flores's ingenious detective-work into the printing of *Don Quixote*, Part I is to put the blame for some of this kind of carelessness on the compositors (Flores 1975). The introduction of Sancho in Chapter 7 – a development prefigured by the innkeeper's advice in Chapter 3 – belongs to the category of happy afterthought. So does the skilful interleaving of episodes from Chapter 23 onwards. This evidently expands the scope of the original design, whatever this may have been: witness the increasingly swollen size of internal 'parts' three and four in relation to one and two. About mid-Part I, the nature of Don Quixote's journey subtly and permanently changes: it becomes less insistently chivalric, more pastoral and Byzantine, more attuned to courtly pastime and humanistic discourse. The hectic pace slackens. Cervantes now presents a leisurely country ride, with halts at more hospitable hostelries, time for civilised talk, for acquaintance with strangers and their stories, and for witnessing other marvels and curiosities. Part II accentuates these tendencies.

Episodes, loosely identified with *cuentos* or *novelas* or *otras digresiones*, are integral to this change. They appear to be a diversion from the novel's essential business; and Cervantes, with his neo-classical aesthetics, encourages this impression by justifying them on grounds of pleasing variety (preambles to I, 28 and II, 44). In II, 44, he refers to the Captive's story and *El curioso impertinente* as being 'as though separate from the history', and implies that the remaining episodes of Part I, though defensible because they impinge on the hero, are insufficiently bound up with him and disproportionately long. These considerations avowedly influence his handling of episodes in Part II. His formulation of them, typically whimsical and humorous, does some injustice to their integral place in the design of the novel.

The first episode in Part I is pastoral and concerns the unrequited love of Grisóstomo, ending in his death, for the cold, beautiful, and wilful Marcela. He reminds us of the obsessively morbid, suicidal lovers of the Spanish courtly love tradition in its bucolic mode. She, robustly rational and eloquent, makes a dramatic appearance at his funeral to rebut his and his friends' recriminations against her, especially the implication that merely by virtue of being the object of a man's love she is under obligation to reciprocate it. The episode has attracted much commentary (e.g. Poggioli 1975), because of the enduring emotiveness of this *cuestión de amor* and its starkly ambivalent dramatisation; the ambivalence concerns *inter alia* Cervantes's attitude to the pastoral genre. Using a technique with precedents in Boccaccio and Bandello, he initially presents the figure of Marcela to us through the prejudiced commentary of her critics, before causing her to appear in a public forum and overturn our prejudices (if not theirs) by her spirited self-defence. One of her critics is the goat-herd Pedro, whose story sets the background to the affair. From his parochial viewpoint, Marcela's resolve to embrace a celibate *vita solitaria* and Grisóstomo's adoption of the life of a love-lorn shepherd for her sake are equally eccentric; and this view of them brings the literary conventionality of their behaviour down to earth with a bump. The effect is reinforced, as far as Grisóstomo is concerned, by Pedro's witty satire of pastoral lamentation, preciosity, and despair:

A shepherd sighs here, another laments there; amatory songs resound yonder, despairing dirges hither. One fellow spends all the hours of the night sitting at the foot of some oak or rock, and there, without having shut his tearful eyes, rapt and transported in his thoughts, he is discovered by the morning sun; another, without allowing his sighs respite or intermission, stretched on the burning sand in the full heat of the summer's most oppressive *siesta*, directs his laments to merciful heaven.

(I, 12; i, 166)

The passage typifies Cervantes's anti-pastoral vein. Moreover, the extravagances of behaviour described in it remind us of Don Quixote, notably his nocturnal vigils; we are thus induced to see him and Grisóstomo as tarred with a similar brush. Pedro's satire complements the moral thrust of Marcela's speech, which undermines the ethical base of the courtly lover's cult of despairing recrimination; and this in turn complements Vivaldo's ironic insinuations in Chapter 13 about the unpracticality and idolatry of the chivalric code. Yet Cervantes's treatment of the pastoral convention is by no means wholly negative. The death of the young, talented Grisóstomo is a human tragedy, even though he brought it on himself. Marcela's claim to enjoy the freedom that is her birthright, in communion with nature and her maker, is stated with eloquent nobility; it accords with the ideals of the epoch's country-praising poetry. And Pedro is a receptive and appropriate informant about this pastoral drama, not merely a comic foil to it; he reacts with curiosity, a sense of wonder and regret; and his homeliness provides an appropriate bridge between Don Quixote's world and the literary theatricality of the funeral.

The episode, from a formal viewpoint, is a landmark in the genre of the novel, particularly the comic novel, and is, in some ways, a model for the treatment of subsequent episodes in *Don Quixote*. The interpolations of serious matter in the picaresque novel *Guzmán de Alfarache* are hived off from the main action, they are recounted as stories by characters involved in it, in a spirit of 'And now for something completely different'. It is a spirit which, in diverse forms, pervades the Renaissance's art of narrative: imitations of the *Decameron*, pastoral romances, Ariosto's *Orlando Furioso*. Cervantes's originality lies in fusing the heterogeneous branch with the main trunk, instead of treating it as detachable. In the episode of Marcela and Grisóstomo, the worlds of low and high pastoral are quite inter-dependent; and the fortunes of Don Quixote and the episode's protagonists mirror each other and intertwine. Of course, we must not exaggerate the extent of Cervantes's achievement; he still persists with the conception of a long narrative as a main 'trunk' with episodic 'branches'. Nor, however, must we belittle it. He made the discovery that the matter of a comic novel need not be restricted to the undignified doings of low characters; it can include any matter taken from any genre, naturalising it by the perspective from which it is considered. He made a further discovery: that the 'branches' can have an organic, rather than merely accidental, relation to the 'trunk'.

Episodes are integral to *Don Quixote's* design because its hero's frustrated efforts to live on a plane of literary heroism naturally call forth a positive complement. His stilted but elegant speech on the Golden Age (I, 11) evokes an Arcadian time when men, nourished by Mother Earth's bounty, lived together in unsophisticated amity, and when simply attired shepherdesses could roam the woods unmolested. The speech's consecrated topoi are pointedly contrasted with its circumstances: a supper with goat-herds, who, despite the roughness of their manners and entertainment – cheese harder than plaster, goat stew, an informally circulated wineskin – have something of Arcadian sincerity of purpose. The speech also serves as a natural portal to the wooded *sierra* where Marcela leads her *vita solitaria*. Engaged in reviving a literary golden age of chivalry, Don Quixote delivers a eulogy of Arms in contrast with Letters: another post-prandial discourse on another humanistic topos (I, 37–38). This is quickly followed by the Captive's story, which evokes a very recent, *historic* age of chivalry and turns thematically on a contrast of vocations: the Captive's and his brother's, Arms and Letters. The circumstances in which the *novela* about the impertinently curious husband is discovered and read out make us consider it as potentially recommendable literature, hence to be contrasted with the chivalric romances which occupy the same locked suitcase (I, 32). Cardenio's mad despair in the *sierra* is deliberately juxtaposed with Don Quixote's burlesque version of it, and calls to mind the prototypes of Amadís and Roland even before Don Quixote explicitly cites them as models of imitation (I, 23–27). Cardenio's plight is provoked by the treachery of his friend Don Fernando, who breaks his pledge to the seduced farmer's daughter, Dorotea, and secretly betroths himself to Cardenio's sweetheart Luscinda. This story of chivalry denied, then grudgingly reaffirmed, proceeds in parallel with Don Quixote's chimerically gallant attempt to restore 'Princess Micomicona', i.e. Dorotea in that burlesque role, to her usurped kingdom. These symmetries are so many ways of proclaiming: 'that's mere literature; here is life' (Riley 1962, chapter 1). They are reinforced by the interleaving and intertwining of the episodes with the main action, and their fragments with each other: all typical of Cervante's Byzantine narrative techniques. They point to underlying moral themes and dilemmas, common to the main action and the episodes, which run through the whole novel and surface more explicitly in Part II than Part I. They, and the whole process of intertwining, produce the tonal complexity that characterises *Don Quixote* and its harmonisation of comedy with graver matters. This tonal variety rests on a basis of continuity: common nature.

Common nature

I borrow this phrase from the Canon of Toledo's splendid invective against the romances of chivalry in I, 49, which includes the assertion that he would cast even the best of them in the fire 'for being false and fraudulent and beyond the pale of common nature' (i, 578). Compliance with that criterion saves the romance *Tirant lo Blanc* from that fate during the scrutiny of Don Quixote's library (I, 6). The priest says of it enthusiastically: 'Here knights eat and sleep and die in their beds and make their wills before dying, and other such things lacking in all other books of this genre' (i, 117). These words have a thematic significance: they are specifically reflected in the circumstances of Don Quixote's death and the scribe's judgement on it (II, 74). As this *libro de caballerías* ends, so it begins: with a detailed account of the hero's routine menu and apparel.

As we have seen, the hero's adventures conform to a pattern whose sheer repetition emphasises certain qualities in the facts of life that he denies, implying not just aesthetic but also ethical criteria that would conform to those facts. I take it that there is an intuitive concept of a natural and rational norm in *Don Quixote* (Mandel 1958), not the quasi-pantheistic one formulated by Castro (1925, chapter 4) but one aligned with Catholic orthodoxy. Though it has an explicitly formulated aspect, the norm is above all implied by non-conceptual means: the materiality of things, how people sleep and eat, 'the facts of the matter', significant contrasts of character. So it is in these areas that we should chiefly look for it.

Flaubert put his finger on an important paradox about *Don Quixote* when he spoke of those roads of Spain which one sees everywhere in it though they are nowhere described. Uncluttered by the characteristic furniture of the realist novel – detailed descriptions of physical ambiance – it is nonetheless vividly photogenic. Why? One can think of various reasons; but perhaps the most important is this: the hero's fertile misapprehensions about phenomena set our imaginations hard at work in order to counter his false yet vivid pictures with likely ones, concordant with the premise that the objects in question are such as one may see any day on the plain of La Mancha in the historical present – the present within the novel's frame of reference. Since the phenomena are given to us in their initially mysterious 'phenomenological' aspect, as clouds of dust or clanks in the night, they make us ask 'What is it?', 'What causes it?', thus taking us back to epistemology's nursery school. The Russian formalists held that the function of art is to make us re-discover the habitual objects of experience, jaded by over-familiarity. *Don Quixote* is a striking illustration of the principle.

Hence, normality and solidity, as opposed to literary fabulousness, are common nature's basic properties. Sancho doubts that those who tossed him in a blanket were phantoms or enchanted persons; they seemed men of flesh-and-blood like ourselves with common-or-garden names (I, 18). Concerning the hero's delirious fantasies of being transported hundreds of leagues across the ocean by enchanted boat, Cervantes quietly observes that the commandeered fishing-boat glided serenely along the Ebro in mid-current, 'without being propelled by any secret intelligence or hidden enchanter, but by the very course of the water, at that moment smooth and gentle' (II, 29; ii, 265).

In discovering normality's comic potential, Cervantes had to resist strong traditional assumptions about the nature of comic subject-matter, which, in the pungent phrase of one of his aesthetic mentors, had to carry the whiff of clumsiness and ugliness (*cf.* Aristotle, *Poetics* 1449a). True, the whiff is powerfully emitted by parts of Don Quixote's world. Yet other parts – e.g. the river Ebro's gentle flow – are not clumsy or ugly at all, or only appear as such in a certain mocking relationship. It is implied that outside that relationship they may merit serious respect, including the right to be considered in realistic proportion.

The implication is manifest in the tone of explanations in the novel: an important feature of it, since it abounds in mysteries requiring clarification. In general, the more elaborate the mystery, the more detailed and factual the explanation. Not even the many leg-pullers in the novel, most notably its narrator, escape this law: a reflection of its underlying concern with verisimilitude. Cervantes keeps us waiting a long time before revealing the identity and guilty secrets of Maese Pedro: revelation, when it comes, is copious, factual, and *sober* (II, 27; *cf*. II, 15, 62, 70). Of course, explanations, whether by the narrator or by the characters, are also offered tongue-in-cheek; they may be replaced by facetious prevarication. Yet except when the facts in question are trivial or preposterous, the veil draped by jest over fact is temporary or transparent. 'Así era la verdad' is a phrase with sacrosanct force in this book.

In *La Galatea*, Cervantes marks temporal divisions by brief, ornamental descriptions of sunrise, sunset, and other phases of the day's cycle, coinciding with the beginnings, endings, or interruptions of the shepherds' activities. He continues the practice in *Don Quixote*, where the descriptions become much more functional. They focus on Don Quixote's and Sancho's reactions to the physical necessities of eating and sleeping, and thus acquire thematic significance; they are also basic to the contrast between the former's highmindedness and the latter's lowmindedness. An early passage of this type occurs in I, 8 and includes a description of how master and squire spend their first night. Don Quixote spent it in sleepless vigil for Dulcinea; not so Sancho, who, as he had his belly full, and not of chicory water, slept obliviously through, 'and had his master not called him, he would not have been woken by the rays of the sun on his face, nor by the song of numerous birds merrily saluting the day's coming' (i, 132). Unlike the parodic dawn-description in I, 2, the mention of sunshine and bird-song here shows no exaggerated preciosity or particular emphasis. They just represent nature's cheering and salutary routine, mocking Sancho's swinish torpor, which in turn mocks his master's romantic vigil. The ironic absurdity of the passage, like that of the Quixote/Sancho relationship in general, rests on a concept of their behaviour as opposed types of excess, in relation to which there is a golden mean. It is stated by Don Quixote in his counsels of government to Sancho: 'Let your sleep be moderate, for he who does not rise with the sun does not enjoy the day' (II, 43; ii, 362).

Master and squire are not excluded from nature's norm on a subsequent occasion: the picnic after the rout of the funeral cortège. The passage illustrates the dynamism of this leitmotif; time here is lived *durée*, space permeates the pores of sense:

And after riding a short distance between two low mountains, they found themselves in a wide secluded valley, where they dismounted, and Sancho unloaded the ass, and reclining on the green grass, with the relish of hunger, they had breakfast, lunch, afternoon snack and supper all in one, satisfying their bellies with more than one picnic hamper that the dead man's escort of priests, who seldom let themselves do badly, had brought with them in the food supplies carried by the pack mule. But another mishap befell them which to Sancho was calamity indeed, and it was that they had no wine to drink, nor even water to raise to their lips; and as they were parched with thirst, Sancho, noting that the meadow where they found themselves was full of short green grass, said what will be related in the next chapter.   (I, 19; i, 236)

The grassy valley suggests the *loci amoeni* of pastoral but has a sensorial immediacy alien to it. The lush grass promises relief to Sancho, so thirsty that he will even settle for water. Soon they hear the welcome din of a mighty cascade, but also, alas, a sinister pounding and clanking 'which cast a wet blanket over their joy'. A new adventure is imminent (see p. 22). The passage just quoted, seemingly a mere bridge between adventures, marks an important change in physical ambiance and recapitulates, in a positive key, a cycle of shared experience. The dominant impression of a very recent adventure, the battle with the sheep, was of dust, heat, haze, and wide empty vistas (I, 18). Now we are in a quite different theatre of action, with different literary associations: in the dark of night, we sense the presence of water, grass, forest, mountainous foothills. Common nature here is not a banal antithesis to the hero's expectations, but a congenial stimulus. The impressive verb-cluster describing the attack on the priests' provisions (the original Spanish is 'almorzaron, comieron, merendaron y cenaron' and means literally, 'breakfasted, lunched, snacked, and dined') reminds us that this has been a long, hungry, and traumatic day; the traumas have been emotional as well as physical. The day's cycle of events ends on an upbeat, with hunger satisfied, morale and saddle bags restored, grassy repose for weary limbs, and, implicitly, growth in intimacy and trust between master and man. The anti-clerical jibe in mid-passage give pragmatic legitimacy to the carefree plunder of stolen food: 'they can afford to lose it'. Yet this glad surrender to the belly's urges contrasts ironically with Don Quixote's normal abstemiousness and also with his principle: 'It is never my custom to despoil those I conquer' (I, 21; i, 256). As usual, chivalry wears the dunce's hat; what is consonant with common nature is shared food and relief, the human bond, the discarding of highfalutin precept. A similar cleavage is apparent in a scene to which we shall revert later: Don Quixote's first moment of humility in Part I is accompanied by a confession of a craving for coarse bread and smoked sardines and by quotations from the Gospel of St Matthew about God's providence. The conjunction is significant: in this book, humble necessities such as hunger are not just mentioned but dignified. They enter into a conception of the whole man, whose fulfilment includes the poetic, moral, social, and religious sides of his nature as well as healthy animal urges.

In a sense, this integral vision was comedy's gift to Cervantes. In his serious fiction conventional scruples of decorum curb this humanising particularity about familiar matters. Just how gloriously comedy broke those shackles is shown by the lyrical yet Gargantuan description of the mouth-watering provisions for Camacho's banquet (II, 20): a roasting bullock spitted on an elm-trunk, infinite game and birds hanging from the trees, cheeses stacked like ramparts, piles of pure white bread heaped like corn in the threshing-ground. All this is a feast for gluttonous Sancho's eyes. Together with the equestrian display, the witty danced masque, the shady bowers, the bridal procession, it reminds us of the idealised rustic weddings in Góngora's *Solitudes* and Lope de Vega's comedies: man harmoniously united to nature in a fitting fulfilment of virtue, beauty, youth, and country custom.

The point is not invalidated by the fact that not all is idyllic serenity and goodwill at Camacho's wedding.

The conceptual basis of this 'philosophy of common nature' is conveniently summed up by Don Quixote's counsels of government to Sancho (II, 42–43): fear of God, self-knowledge, humility, preference of virtue to false honour, justice, temperance, charity, a sense of propriety, loyalty to family. They reflect the novel's general emphasis on lay, domestic, middle-class values, which contrasts with the more heroic, aristocratic tendency of Lope de Vega's theatre and is exemplified by the promise: 'If you follow these precepts and rules, Sancho, your days will be long, your fame eternal, your rewards overflowing, your happiness indescribable; you will marry your children as you wish, they and your grandchildren will have titles, you will live in peace and benevolence with your fellow-men' (II, 42; ii, 360). Tirsi, praising good love in *La Galatea* Book 4, asserts the goodness of all the natural drives implanted in man by his maker, from the physical to the rational. One of those that *Don Quixote* repeatedly upholds is natural bent: to marry or not to marry, write poetry, go to war. The eighteenth-century English novelists well appreciated Cervantes's sympathy for amiable eccentricity. So this ethics is not narrow or exclusive. One of its axioms is 'Vive la différence!'

There is a creative tension between this and another axiom: a sense of fitness, which is not equivalent to prudent circumspection but rather to the Preacher's reminder: 'To every thing there is a season.' Don Quixote admonishes the governor-elect to avoid using proverbs indiscriminately, holding himself on a horse as though it were an ass, eating garlic, making invidious comparisons of lineages, belching or – even worse – saying 'burp'. These admonitions imply the reasons for Sancho's comic appeal: he is a living-and-breathing infraction of each one of them. A sense of fitness goes together with measuring aspirations to capacity, not asking of nature more than it can give, respect for social custom, compliance with providence's decrees. Within that framework,

one can be forger of one's destiny (II, 65), and heroic idealism
and altruistic endeavour have their place.

The pattern of Don Quixote's adventures implies a validation
of mature reason as opposed to various kinds of impulsive
irrationality. These are the butts ridiculed in Cervantes's comedies and farces: superstition, jealousy, self-indulgent heroics,
crackbrained ambition, symptoms of the insatiable desire which
is the condition of fallen human nature. Another lesson of Don
Quixote's failures is this: though nature holds many secrets,
Providence moves in mysterious ways, and life-in-society and the
human soul are often deceptive; nevertheless life's problems,
which are essentially moral, are decipherable by reason aided by
experience. 'One must set one's hand to appearances to free
oneself of error', says the hero, taking a small but significant step
towards the recovery of sanity (II, 11; ii, 117; *cf.* Parker 1956).

Yet *Don Quixote*, in deference to the decorum of comedy
(prologue to Part I), does not sermonise. Even the apparent
sermons, like the counsels of government, are set in light, comic,
idiosyncratic perspective. The 'moral philosophy' sketched above
is the latent sense of the novel's comedy. 'When leniency could
and should have its place, do not apply all the rigour of the law
to the delinquent' (II, 42; ii, 359). This, another of the precepts
given to Sancho, is nowhere stated in the episode of the galley-
slaves (I, 21). Yet it is a hidden presupposition of the comic
opposition of extremes that the adventure presents: Don Quixote's Utopian forgiveness versus the convicts' nonchalant cyni-
cism, according to which the only crime is not to have enough
bribe money, spirit to lie under torture, friends in the right places.
Having failed to move the guards by his eloquence, Don Quixote
liberates the convicts by force and is rewarded by them with a
hail of stones. Cervantes ends the chapter with a picture of two
horizontal figures and two vertical ones; the latter pair includes
the ass, whose ears, twitching in reflex response to the now con-
cluded pelting, offer the nearest thing to a moral comment on
the outcome. As does the episode of Marcela and Grisóstomo,
this adventure presents a starkly dramatic contrast of attitudes to

a moral problem, here unstated; the effect is rather like that of casting a weighty stone into a deep pool. Ripples of implication are created; and the discreet reader is left to meditate on them. The changed nature of episodes in Part II intensifies this effect.

Form of Part II; its episodes

Don Quixote Part II differs from Part I in structure and mood. Critical discussions of chivalric and contemporary literature drop out and the comic battering-ram loses some of its polemical vigour. The adventures which hinge on the hero's chivalric fantasies tend to be developed on a larger scale and to be more interconnected than the casual, independent roadway encounters of the first two sallies. These changes are accompanied by important modifications of the hero's psychology, to be discussed later. For the moment, I wish to concentrate on the 'episodes' of Part II, insofar as they can be distinguished from the adventures. To do so, we must take account of Part II's atmosphere, particularly as it affects the relationship of the two heroes to other people.

Part II transpires in holiday mood; the season is springtime/ early summer; this is a Green World largely removed from urban and courtly bustle; it teems with entertainers, people in costume, adventurers, social outcasts. These types are different from the ones encountered in Part I: more exotic than those obscure wayfarers engaged in daily pursuits and more in touch with public, historical reality than those heroes and heroines of sentimental romance. The novel's greater topical reference is explained in a general way, by the invasion of the hero's world by Benengeli's readership. He meets actors of the troupe of Angulo el Malo (II, 11), the Catalan brigand Roque Guinart (II, 60), a page-boy disillusioned with his treatment at court and travelling to join the army (II, 24). While entertained at a Duke's country-seat in Aragon, he is given a taste of high-society life, including the pageant and perils of a boar-hunt (II, 34). At Barcelona, he is received on board a Spanish war-galley and finds himself unexpectedly involved in pursuit of a Turkish pirate ship (II, 63).

Sancho, in Barataria, walks the corridors of power (II, 45 ff.). The two heroes are feted at a lavish country-wedding (II, 20) and watch a folksy puppet-show at a rural inn (II, 26). Sequences of talk and incident are grouped in cycles, whose basis is either the sightseeing itinerary or something like 'the country-house weekend'. Less single-minded about their chivalric mission, the heroes rather resemble tourists on a protracted jaunt. Don Quixote, his fame secured by Benengeli's chronicle, has time for marvelling at other people's experiences and commenting on them. Thanks to his recurrent lucid intervals, this commentary is heard with respect; it ranges over the epoch's significant moral/ social agenda: honour, marriage, education, government, the rights of war. Because the strangers who meet him and Sancho are effectively or potentially their fan-club, their attitudes also include hospitality, friendliness, urbanity, acclaim, discreetly dis- simulated mirth and astonishment – rather different from the amused or pitying condescension with which they were formerly treated.

The question of what constitutes an episode in Part II is prob- lematic; different authorities come up with different lists. Since the episodes of Part II represent, in my view, the zenith of Cer- vantes's art of comic fiction, the question is no mere technicality. The upshot of Cervantes's vaguely worded explanation of his change of policy towards them is this: in Part II he has decided not to introduce detachable *novelas* like those of Part I, but certain episodes resembling them, arising directly out of the main story and expressed as succinctly as may be (II, 44). Armed with these guidelines, one will probably draw up a list shorter than that intended by him, since there are relatively few episodes which match the description. They include Ana Félix's story (II, 63), Camacho's wedding (II, 19–21), the story of the braying alder- man (II, 25), Claudia Jerónima's story (II, 60), and arguably one or two others. Whichever set one chooses, one is faced with baffling problems of discrimination. If the story of the beautiful *morisca* Ana Félix counts as an episode, so must its precursor: her father's account of his family's and community's sufferings in exile (II, 54). Yet this, when related, has the appearance of a socially representative testimony rather than a *novela*. Why should we not also include the testimony of the Catalan highwayman Roque Guinart and the scene depicting his Robin Hood-like liberality (II, 60)? They are adjacent to Claudia Jerónima's story, and though just as episodic are in no way novelesque. What of Sancho's governorship? Is this – including all the cases, stories, and testimonies it contains – an episode? The timing of Cervantes's explanation of his policy-change, just prior to the governorship, suggests that it may be. Such questions are made possible because Cervantes has been as good as his word: he has blurred the distinction between 'branch' and 'trunk'. He has also, I suspect, changed his conception of the nature of the 'branch' in line with his practice in *Persiles* Book III, composed at about the same time as *Don Quixote* Part II. Both works feature numerous digressive sequences of talk or incident in which the limelight turns from the principals and falls on other characters' lives, interests, and pursuits, seen in a genially satiric light as often as in a romantic one, and presented via brief self-portraits or informal dialogue as often as through stories. In practice, any such sequence may be considered 'episodic'.

The heterogenous matter of episodes in Part II – politics, pastoral masques, apologues, village-theatricals, and much else – is unified by the fact that it is presented for the meditation and commentary of the two heroes and furthers their moral evolution. Thanks to this dual, unifying perspective, Cervantes is able skilfully to vary the tone and matter of these episodes, while harmonising them with pre-existing motifs, and also, to make the strangers featured in them shed the scales of stereotype and reveal themselves with a marvellous blend of naturalness, humanity, humour and unselfconsciousness. Two brief examples may illustrate the point about unity-in-variety. The encounter with the Catalan brigand Roque Guinart is tense and dramatic; his style of life, as he points out to Don Quixote, might be considered a kind of knight-errantry; it illustrates where the motive to 'vengar agravios' (to right offences) leads in practice: an abyss of disquiet, fear, and violence. The point has just previously been made by the sudden appearance of the dashingly attired Claudia Jerónima, who pours out, with hectic brevity, the tragic story of how she has just shot her own lover in a fit of jealousy, after hearing of his plan to marry another woman. Claudia and Roque then catch up with the mortally wounded Don Vincente, who just has time before expiring to tell his mistress that she acted on a false rumour. Several chapters before (II, 25), the theme of 'righting offences' has been illustrated in an altogether different key by the story of the braying aldermen, who made perfect asses of themselves by revelling in their virtuoso capacity to imitate an ass's bray. The story, told with superb comic polish by a man from their village, has a Sanchopanzine flavour by virtue of its folkloric associations and its theme of rustic nitwittedness. The ending speaks of sinister consequences: war between the 'braying' village and those who have dubbed it with this attribute. In the sequel (II, 27), by means of an affable and learned lecture on the conditions of the just war, Don Quixote tries to dissuade the army of braying villagers from seeking revenge in a futile cause. His familiar expertise on the military code is here tuned in a lucid key. Rustic comedy is thus elevated to a reflective level, before collapsing in undignified farce when Sancho endorses his master's speech with an inopportune imitation of an ass's bray, and incurs the predictable consequences.

As these examples indicate, the episodes of Part II are treated loosely as mirror-images of the two heroes' experience; in this respect, they resemble those of Part I, which reflect Don Quixote's. They tend to be presented in the mutely suggestive, dramatically contrasted fashion previously noted. They thus assume a significance which is not merely self-contained but reciprocal; each one may be seen as part of a constellation of related cases which throw light on the central, perennial dilemmas posed by Don Quixote's behaviour: heart or head?; Arms or Letters?; discretion or valour?; heroic adventurousness or stay-at-home conformism?

I propose to illustrate this in detail with reference to Don

Quixote's encounter with Don Diego de Miranda (II, 16–18), which includes 'episodic' material – notably, Don Diego's self-portrait. This gentleman, encountered on the highway, is described as middle-aged, handsomely attired in green, with a grave yet cheerful face; Don Quixote is struck by his appearance and deems him a man of substance. Don Diego reveals that he is a well-to-do farmer, who spends his life amongst his family, friends, and neighbours; he hunts in a modest way, presides over a clean, quiet, and well-ordered household, enjoys giving hospitality, and has a library of some six dozen books. He shuns malicious gossip, vainglory, and hypocrisy, shares his goods with the poor, and is a devotee of the Virgin. The same ideal of virtuous contentment in rural seclusion, contrasted with the busy turmoil of the court, runs insistently through the writings of Cervantes's contemporaries. It is indirectly validated by Sancho's renunciation of the governorship and by Don Quixote's of chivalry. I have no doubt that Don Diego is meant to be seen as an exemplary figure.

This view is not shared unanimously by Cervantine critics (e.g. Márquez Villanueva 1975). In mentioning this, my purpose is less to urge my view against its opponents than to draw attention to the reasons why the episode is capable of provoking such differing reactions. They have much to do with *Don Quixote's* reverbating power of implication. Don Diego's self-portrait is elicited by Don Quixote's more flamboyant and self-promoting one, and is quite pointedly contrasted with it. Chivalry books have *no* place on his library shelves: a detail which suggests that Don Diego is an ideal, up-market version of what the hero might have been but for his literary obsession. Yet the episode's purpose is not corrective but celebratory: it dramatises the extraordinariness of the hero's personality, and especially its intriguing blend of lunacy and lucidity, by portraying the astonished reactions to him of a discreet person who, exceptionally in Part II, has not read Benengeli's 'chronicle'. In picking that person, Cervantes shows nice dramatic flair: there could hardly be a more significant arbiter. We should be careful, however, to distinguish between fascination and emotional or ethical identification; in Don Diego's case, the first attitude stops well short of the second.

Don Quixote's claim to have revived the order of chivalry as described in chivalry books initially causes his interlocutor to doubt his sanity (II, 16); but these suspicions are virtually dispelled by Don Quixote's eloquent lecture on the nobility of poetry and the advisability of letting children follow their natural bent. It is prompted by his learning of the literary enthusiasm of Don Diego's son, a student at Salamanca, who, in his father's view, wastes time on poetry that should be devoted to more serious pursuits. We discover here an opposition between poetic enthusiasm and middle-brow prudence, youthful impulsiveness and parental restraint; this kind of opposition is recurrent in the novel. Cast characteristically as champion of enthusiasm, Don Quixote appears to have a cultural broad-mindedness that Don Diego lacks. Now an incident occurs which revives the latter's suspicions with full vigour (II, 17).

They encounter a cart bearing two fierce lions in a cage: a gift from the general of the garrison of Oran to His Majesty. To Don Diego's consternation, Don Quixote reacts as though the lions had been sent as a personal challenge to him by enemies, no doubt enchanters, intent on testing his mettle: 'Lion-whelps at me? At me, and at such an hour? By God, the gentlemen who send them here will see if I'm a man to be frightened by lions!' (II, 17; ii, 160). The gesture is firmly characterised as one of paranoid and puerile bravado. At the beginning of the chapter, after he and his travelling-companion had sighted a cart showing royal pennants, Don Quixote began muttering darkly about needing to be prepared at any moment for the attacks of unseen enemies. Then, in case we miss the point, Cervantes contrives some heavy symbolism. He causes the hero to clap on his head a helmet that Sancho has just used as shopping-bag for some curds; when squashed matter starts oozing down his cheeks he wonders whether his brains have addled. The build-up to the fight is a superb example of Cervantes's technique of tantalisingly yet humorously inflating a balloon of suspense prior to anti-climax.

Don Diego's rational remonstrations, the lion-keeper's legalistic announcement that any damage resulting from the opening of the cage will be Don Quixote's responsibility, Sancho's tearful pleas, Don Quixote's supercilious reactions to such admonitions, Benengeli's ironically over-blown panegyric to him just prior to the moment of battle – all serve to delay the fateful moment. When it comes, the balloon crumples absurdly. The king of beasts yawns, licks its face like a fireside tabby, turns its hind quarters to the challenger, and lies down again. Cervantes's phrase about the generous lion's courteous disdain for childish bravado reveals clearly whom he regards as the true hero of this affair.

Though the contest was abortive, Don Quixote gloats over his moral victory. The lionkeeper, no doubt anxious to keep his charges safe, and exhorted by Don Quixote to render a glowing testimony of his courage and the lion's cowardice, duly does so; the tip of one gold *escudo* provides incentive to hyperbole. Don Quixote treats the outcome as proof that the wiles of enchantment are unavailing against true valour; clearly, he does not just wish to prove a point to Don Diego, as he had implied in II, 16, but to prove one to himself after recent frustrations (see p. 29). Then, while Don Diego is inwardly pondering the astonishing contradictions of his behaviour, Don Quixote addresses a speech of self-justification to him, answering Don Diego's previous admonition that rashness is not courage but lunacy. The speech is stylish, formal, emotive, satiric, and, at the end, speciously rational. It turns on the contrast between the obligations of the courtier and the knight-errant. The former's talents and functions – skill in tourneys, gallantries to the ladies, conspicuous adornment of a royal court – are noted and damned with faint praise. The latter's obligations – succouring widows in wild places, entering labyrinths, battling with monsters – are extolled in contrastingly grandiose terms. The speech concludes with ingenious casuistry borrowed from Aristotle's *Nicomachaean Ethics*: though true valour consists in a mean between rashness and cowardice, it is better to err on the side of excess than of deficiency. It is another of Don Quixote's virtuoso set-pieces in which many glimmerings of sense are blended with nonsense in disconcertingly elevated style. Don Diego's brief, urbane, yet witheringly ironic rejoinder ought to put the matter in perspective for the discreet reader. Yet for many modern readers, it does not have this effect. Why not?

Cervantes's narration of the adventure is, in a comic sense, highly dramatic; and this highlights the peril of Don Quixote's act and non-committally creates a variety of viewpoints on it, which range from the admiring to the sceptical. The hero's rejoinder to Don Diego's remonstration, with its allusion to his style of hunting, is superbly tart: 'Go and mind your tame decoy partridge and bold ferret and let each person attend to his own business' (II, 17; ii, 161). Is this to be interpreted as supercilious bravado or as a well-aimed rebuke? The lionkeeper's flattery of him astutely tickles his vanity and sense of punctilio: 'Your greatness of heart is already manifest: no brave combatant, as I see it, is obliged to do more than challenge his enemy and await him in the field; if he does not present himself, his is the infamy and the other wins the crown of victory' (ii, 164). Yet it might be read as the admiring testimony of a first-hand witness. The second reason, or set of reasons, is even more important. Don Quixote's speech of self-justification, and his relationship to Don Diego in general seems to invite us to contrast two vocations and to ponder something like the question: Does heroic virtue lie down the path of all-or-nothing adventurousness or its opposite? It taps a strong current of sympathetic approval in the novel for the military life as contrasted with the less active professions, chief amongst them in Part II, the courtier's. In II, 1 Don Quixote declares that on the bodies of present-day knights one is more likely to hear the rustle of damasks than the creak of chain-mail; in II, 24 he meets and approves the ex-page who, on his way to enlist, declares that he would rather serve his king on the battle-field than as a stingy seeker of preferment at court.

We should note, however, that Don Diego's way of life, though sedentary, is just as much opposed to the courtier's as Don Quixote's. Moreover, the idealisation of arms in the novel is tinged by a nostalgic, middle-aged perspective; it is implied that this is a young man's option. When real military adventures present themselves, Don Quixote is shown in an ineffectual and marginal light (II, 60, 63, 65). And his attempted provocation of the lion must be seen in relation to an even more potent current of feeling than the one just mentioned, tending to counter and qualify it: the novel's insistent disapproval of empty belligerence, the picking of quarrels in futile causes. Don Quixote's self-justificatory speech to Don Diego will be decisively refuted by his own explanation of the conditions of the just war in II, 27. Another refutation occurs much later. A sea-chase after a Turkish brigantine ends in its capture, but not before two drunken Turkish soldiers, at the moment of surrender, pointlessly shoot two Spaniards on the pursuing galley (II, 63). The brigantine's captain is asked angrily: 'Aren't you aware that valour is not the same as rashness? Uncertain hopes of success should make men bold, but not foolhardy' (ii, 526). This is not an effete courtier speaking, but a seasoned naval commander. Don Quixote's adventures in Part I provide spectacular cautionary proof of this precept. Thus, it is decidedly not part of Cervantes's ethical thinking to treat heroics as a necessary concomitant of heroism; it insistently distinguishes between excess and mean, the principle and the circumstances of application. I suspect that he would have dismissed the stark ethical alternative posed above as a crude simplification. However – and this is the point that I wish to stress – the dialectical opposition of life-styles in the episode involving Don Diego is not explicitly resolved; it is simply presented and left to the discreet reader's judgement.

Chapter 2

The personalities of Quixote and Sancho

Don Quixote, as considered so far, appears to have the loosely articulated unity of a string of beads. Yet the experience of Quixote and Sancho, as distilled in their conversations, provides unity of a more organic kind: that which we find in many classic novels thematically concerned with forging and losing illusions. The editor of the Penguin edition of Jane Austen's *Pride and Prejudice* has defined its action as 'the fact that a man changes his manners and a young lady changes her mind'. *Don Quixote* is susceptible of similar encapsulation: 'how Sancho learned to live without an island and Don Quixote to die without Dulcinea'.

A glance at the novel shows that much of it is occupied with uneventful talk between the two heroes. Cervantes's motive in giving it such prominence is clearly attested by those who over-hear the conversations (e.g. II, 2 and 7). He wants to project the two heroes as comic 'characters' – bundles of extravagant delusions, bees-in-the-bonnet, mannerisms – and to make his novel revolve around them. Hence the extraordinary shift of attention that he effects, in the context of the history of prose fiction, from incident to dialogue. His primary model consists of the master/servant dialogues of sixteenth-century Spanish comedy in its various species: typically, high/low antiphonals in which the master's rhetorical effusions and posturings of passion and honour are met by the servant's objections, quips, complaints, and concern for his skin and creature comforts. Thoughts of fur-nishing the novel with the thematic unity described above were, no doubt, originally remote from Cervantes's mind; they remain remote in Part I, which ends with two heroes' illusions vigorously alive. They do not begin to crystallise until Part II, where Don Quixote's love for Dulcinea and Sancho's ambitions for the governorship reach a crisis, precipitating disillusion. Yet in writing Part II, Cervantes harmonises the psychological evolution of his two heroes with their experience in Part I; the two Parts thus portray a continuous process.

An example of this microscopic focus on traits, particularly typical of Part I, is the sequel to the quarrel between Don Quixote and Cardenio over the latter's slur on the honour of Queen Madásima (end of Chapter 24). Cardenio accuses the Queen of having been the mistress of her surgeon, Elisabat. Both are minor, unconnected figures in *Amadís de Gaula*; popular tradition may have been the source of Cardenio's 'libel' (see Murillo's edition, i, 298). The quarrel is quite insane since the bone of contention is fictitious. Cervantes comments on his hero's part in it: 'How extraordinary! He stood up for her just as if she had been his true and natural liege lady; such was the grip his cursed books had on him' (end of Chapter 24). He begins Chapter 25 with a conversation obviously intended to explore this trait further, in contrast with Sancho's reaction to it. The exchanges are notable for their familiar flavour: one is reminded of bickering between husband and wife on the theme: Why did you have to say that to so-and-so – there was no need to interfere? This is suggested by the ironic references to familiar mannerisms and a shared past, the ripples of altercation disguising latent sympathy and dependence, the petty shows of pique and ploys of one-up-manship. The dialogue's sensitivity to mood and register highlights these qualities. It operates two kinds of comic mechanism: 'quirks' and 'situations'. Of the second, irony of incongruity and Bergsonian repetition (e.g. trait revealed as tic) are so basic and recurrent that I shall not trouble to signal them. To save space I have translated the more significant sections of the passage and abridged and paraphrased the remainder, *marking the abridgements in italics*. What I chiefly want to show is how it pits extreme against extreme and reveals both men united in a common innocence. Sancho reveals something lower than robust common sense. It is happy-go-lucky, plebeian indifference to nice points of honour, aggravated by resentment of yet another painful mishap, the drubbing by Cardenio. Insisting on his point, Don Quixote reveals ridiculously exaggerated gallantry, still smouldering bombast, and prolix delight in reminiscing about his favourite fiction. Neither character is aware of the quarrel's essential inanity or of incurring 'pot calls kettle black' by the unselfconscious references to Cardenio as mad. Sancho's function of puncturing his master's self-conceit is more inadvertent than deliberate and takes the primary form of unworthy contrast of attitude or insistence on unpalatable facts – ironic from the reader's enlightened viewpoint rather than the puncturer's.

Chafing under his master's recent restriction on his freedom of speech (imposed in I, 20), Sancho launches the conversation with this melodramatic request (I, 25; i, 300 ff.):

'Sir, will you please give me your blessing and licence to return home [quirk: disloyalty; situation: heavy hint]. *At least I can chat to my wife and children to my heart's content* [quirk: loquacity]. *Trailing night and day through this wilderness in search of adventure with no reward save kicks, blanketings, brickbats, and punches, and having to keep one's mouth shut is like being buried alive* [quirk: plaintiveness].

Don Quixote grants provisional licence to Sancho, who continues:

Good enough, let's make hay while the sun shines [loquacity].*What was the point of your standing up for the Queen thingummy Magimasa, and who cares whether that priest* [i.e., *abad* for Elisabat] *was her lover or not* [quirks: plebeian insensitivity; solecisms]? *If only you had let it pass, the madman would have got on with his story and we would have been spared the beating-up.*

Don Quixote [warmly, indignation reviving]:

If you knew what an honourable lady Queen Madásima was, you would have said that I showed great patience in not punching the man in the mouth [quirk: fiction treated as history]. *A queen the mistress of a surgeon? Blasphemy!* [exaggerated scruple]. *The truth is that Master Elisabat was the queen's doctor and tutor and a very prudent counsellor to her, but to suggest that there was anything more in their relationship is absurd* [exaggerated propriety, literary obsession]. *The proof is that Cardenio was out of his mind when he said it* [situation: pot/kettle].

Sancho:

Precisely, there was no need to pay attention to a madman [hoist with own petard]. *If that stone had connected with your head instead of your chest, a fine mess we'd be in now.*

At this, Don Quixote pompously lays down the law:

'A knight-errant is obliged to defend women, whoever they may be, against the imputations of all men, sane or insane, especially queens of such excellent wise and worth as Queen Madasima [quirks: crazy punctilio; legalistic register; chivalric archaism of 'tan alta guisa y pro'], to whom I'm particularly attached for her good qualities, for, besides being comely [quirks: archaic *fermosa*; literary obsession], she was also very prudent and long-suffering in her calamities, of which she endured many; and during them the counsels and companionship of Master Elisabat were a great benefit and consolation to her, enabling her to bear her misfortunes wisely and patiently. Hence the ignorant and malicious vulgar found occasion to allege that she was his mistress; and [bombast] they lie, I repeat, all who think or say it lie two hundredfold.'

'You needn't look at me', Sancho answered. 'Their sins are their own affair, say I [proverb: 'allá se lo hayan, con su pan se lo coman', meaning literally 'let them keep it and eat it with their bread']. If they were lovers or not, they will have answered to God for it by now. I've just come from my vines, I know nothing [proverb, implying an alibi]. I'm not one to stick my nose into other men's lives. He who buys and lies about the price feels the pinch in his own purse [proverb against those whose deceptions hurt themselves]. Besides, naked I came into the world, and naked I am now; I've neither lost nor won [Sancho's favourite proverb: 'desnudo nací, desnudo me hallo; ni pierdo ni gano', implying indifference to misfortune]. And if they were lovers, what's that to me? Besides, folk often think there's bacon in the larder and there aren't even poles to hang it on (see p. 29). But who can bolt and bar the open field? They even spoke ill of God.'

This, the first of Sancho's torrents of haphazardly connected proverbs, provokes from his master a reaction of fastidious exasperation soon to become familiar. The irritant effect is compounded by Sancho's happy-go-lucky permissiveness, so very different from what his master's previous formulation of precept required. Proverbs in the Spanish Golden Age had an earthy, colloquial flavour and, often, a malicious humour unmatched by their dull English equivalents. Hence their frequent use by writers to characterise comically plebeian figures and endow them with a corresponding register and outlook. Thus, the contrast in attitude between the two quoted speeches is intensified by style. After a further attempt by Don Quixote to put his impertinent chatterbox of a servant in his place, the dialogue moves on to another topic.

Were the conversations merely a means of pulling comic levers they would quickly pall. Yet the operation of those levers gives each passage of dialogue, despite its apparent meander, a focus, climax, and structure, and also fulfils the further purpose of answering the questions 'why?', 'how?', 'what happens next?', on which the readability of novels depends. Thanks to the conversations, we obtain an intimate and familiar focus on Don Quixote's enterprise; thus it acquires an aspect of lifelike possibility, neatly pinpointed by Dr Johnson's remark concerning him and his squire: 'very few readers, amidst their mirth or their pity, can deny that they have admitted visions of the same kind, though they have not perhaps expected events equally strange, or by means equally inadequate'. We become intrigued as to how the Don will resolve each successive conflict between his delusion and reality: shoring it up with *ad hoc* precedents or principles, finding specious corroboration in particular circumstances – all this accompanied by the familiar psychology of one committed to appearing infallible, dignified, and successful. E.M. Forster's distinction in *Aspects of the Novel* between 'flat' and 'round' characters is pertinent here: 'The test of a round character is whether it is capable of surprising in a convincing way. If it fails to surprise, it is flat' (1961, p. 75). Quixote and Sancho would no doubt be 'flat' – i.e., types of caricatures – if their conversations merely consisted in the predictable repetition of quirks as tics. However, a propensity to change surprisingly is intrinsic to them; and this is largely due to their sensitivity to recent and to cumulat-

ive experience. Memory is an active ingredient of their relationship. So too is aspiration. As the prospect of achievement recedes
or draws nearer, so the barometer of morale rises or falls, and
changes take place in their attitudes to each other and to the
world. These accumulated shifts constitute the novel's inner
drama.

Thus, after the disastrous battle with the sheep (I, 18), Don
Quixote, showing very poor timing, consoles Sancho with a little
homily on the swings and roundabouts of fortune, ending with
the admonition not to be so despondent about misfortunes which
do not directly affect him. Since Sancho has just discovered the
loss of his saddle bags and is inwardly vowing to return home,
the homily provokes from him this retort (i, 225–26):

'How do you mean?. . .Who was the one they tossed in the blanket
yesterday if not my father's son? And my saddle bags, missing today,
with all my valuables in them, whose are they if not his also?'
'Are your saddle bags missing, then, Sancho?', asked Don Quixote.
'That's right', replied Sancho.
'In that case, we've got nothing to eat today', replied Don Quixote.
'Only if. . .there were any shortage in the fields round here of those
herbs that you claim to know about, with which unfortunate knights
errant like you make up for such deficiencies.'
'All the same. . .I would rather have a hunk of bread or some coarse
bran bread and a brace of smoked sardines than all the herbs described
by Dioscorides, even if it were in Dr Laguna's illustrated edition. But
anyway, get on your ass, good Sancho, and follow me, for God, provider
of all things, won't fail us, especially as we're so much employed in his
service, for he doesn't fail the flies of the air nor the worms of the ground
nor the tadpoles of the water, and he is so merciful that he causes his
sun to shine on good and bad alike and his rain to fall on the just and
the unjust.'

Sancho's insubordinate sarcasm in this passage, the most
flagrant symptom so far, is a symptom of his disillusionment.
Don Quixote had said in I, 10 that since knights-errant wandered
through country places, their most likely sustenance consisted of
wild plants and herbs, and for this purpose they needed to be
expert herbalists, as he was. Sancho now taunts him with the

claim. This moment is a turning point for Sancho because it represents an erosion of his initial confidence in his master; when such sarcasm recurs, particularly in Part II, it is a concomitant of the recognition of his master's madness (e.g. II, 10) and the emptiness of his promises and his enterprise (II, 28). Yet its sporadic nature betrays its shallowness; simple-minded credulity, loyalty, affection, or covetous hope soon reassert their grip (see, e.g. II, 28 and 33). So the principle of change in Sancho's personality, partly equivalent to the chastening of experience, is counterbalanced by a principle of continuity. They answer each other like return swings of a pendulum with the result that 'plus ça change, plus c'est la même chose'. The above-cited passage in I, 18 represents rock bottom for Sancho in Part I. A series of morale-raising events follows, including the discovery of the gold coins in the *sierra* (I, 23) and the prospect of his master's marriage to 'Princess Micomicona' (I, 29). Yet they too are interspersed with disillusionments. By the end of Part I the will-o'-the-wisp of the island is as elusive as ever. Though the agenda of the conversation in Part I is devoted in general to Don Quixote's *caballerías*, the chief item on it is Sancho's reward; and this fact alone indicates the dialogue's prosaic and familiar bias, continually subjecting Don Quixote's ideal to ironic distortion.

The passage in I, 18 is an important turning-point for Don Quixote, too. In response to Sancho's sarcasm he displays unprecedented humility, self-mocking humour, and Biblical wisdom – the latter unmarred by the slide down the Chain of Being of the birds of the air and lilies of the field. This anticipates the peaceableness and recurrent lucidity which characterise his conduct in Part II. Yet at this stage such enlightenment is still far away. Even very late in Part II, the revival of his old enthusiasms and combativeness shows that in his case, as in Sancho's, though to a lesser extent than in Sancho's, 'plus ça change . . .'.

I have spoken so far as though the evolution of the two characters were purely to be explained in natural psychological terms. In two important ways it is artificial: the result of 'functional transference' and 'fugal repetition'; by skilful characterisation

Cervantes succeeds in naturalising such artifices. This may for the moment be exemplified by reference to 'functional transference'. In Part II it becomes generally recognised that Sancho's habit of citing proverbs in indiscriminate profusion is intrinsic to his make-up. We have just looked at the first example of it: in Chapter 25 of Part I. Sancho's first, isolated proverb occurs in Chapter 19. One might ask why, if the trait is congenital, it is not displayed much earlier. The answer is obvious: it only occurred to Cervantes in mid-Part I that this stereotyped function of low, comic characters might become an agreeable ornament of Sancho's. So, willy-nilly, he grafts it on Sancho's character, where it sits quite naturally: a fitting extension of his already well-established talkativeness and down-to-earth rusticity. Likewise, Don Quixote's lucid interval about bread and sardines marks a new role for him: that of sententious *raisonneur*. This might seem odd in a madman, were it not for the fact that his crazily applied eloquence and learning already contain it potentially.

Quixote's burlesque character

Don Quixote's character, which is displayed through the conversations (not just those with Sancho), has a burlesque nucleus. Though Cervantes does not use the equivalent terms for burlesque or parody (except incidentally in *DQ* II, 22), the concepts that they express match both his practice and his understanding of it. Subsequent practitioners or theorists of burlesque – Sorel, Scarron, Butler, Addison, Pope, Fielding – regarded him as a model. So I have no qualms about interpreting his novel from this perspective. I propose to treat burlesque and parody as interchangeable terms and to offer a definition compatible both with contemporary usage and with literary practice in 'the Classical Age'. The genre's essential features are: mimicry of a literary form in a manner which may vary from predominantly 'high' (matched in gravity to the original) to 'low' (overtly coarser than it), and from lightly playful to debunkingly aggressive, and with a comic effect which depends on some exaggerated incongruity involving style, matter, status of characters. Examples are: Folengo's Virgilian hexameters speckled with pseudo-Latin *vocabulazzi* of vernacular origin; Scarron's Virgilian heroes speaking like Parisian *bourgeois* or tradesmen. A strong sense of the decorum appropriate to genres and social levels underlies these Classical examples of burlesque. Cervantes shares it. The definition just offered squares with what Cervantes repeatedly says about his hero: e.g. his scrupulous imitativeness; the ludicrous dissonance between his style and the addressees. Though the imitation is not as scrupulous as he asserts, this does not invalidate the point that he wants it to create that impression. Only one other general consideration is pertinent. Burlesque, like irony, usually depends on being recognised as some kind of meta-discourse. *Don Quixote's* peculiarity in this respect is that it relies on such recognition in a vague, attentuated form.

To see how Cervantes gets away with it, we may begin by noting that he brings off parody's violent dislocations with a lifelikeness that Henry Fielding, for one, thought impossible. Fielding's opinions on the matter are worthy of attention. He wrote his *Joseph Andrews* (1742) in imitation of the manner of Cervantes and gave his reasons, in the preface, why he had admitted burlesque in the narrator's diction (i.e. the manner) while excluding it from the protrayal of character. Since the latter demands the just imitation of nature and since burlesque always involves 'appropriating the manners of the highest to the lowest, or *è converso*', the two are quite incompatible. So Fielding thought, and we might be inclined to agree with him. Burlesque, because of its violent disjunctions, normally requires a flight into fantasy. Thus, the final scene of *The Life of Brian*, a parody of a Hollywood Biblical epic by the Monty Python team, shows the crucified prisoners resigning themselves to their fate with the rendering of the cheerful ditty 'Always look on the bright side'. In more than one sense, we are not supposed to take this seriously. Cervantes might conceivably have gone down the path to wonderland; he does so in certain parts of *Don Quixote* (e.g. the story of the Cave of Montesinos) and in his *Voyage to Parnassus*, which treats its mythological subject in a familiarly reductive, jocularly fantastic way. That he does not adopt this procedure in most of *Don Quixote* has to do with its critical objective and its concern with verisimilitude. Instead, he chooses a mode of burlesque whose vehicle is, precisely, 'character'. He makes the monstrous disjunctions of burlesque appear natural by giving them a psychological root in the hero's mind. He achieves them, initially at least (see p. 14), by effecting a clash between that mind and the types of behaviour and milieu – notably, society's basement areas – that the epoch considered as being quintessentially comic.

From the outset the hero's imitation has an improvisatory quality, like that of an actor with no precise text to follow, but general guidelines of character and style to develop *ad lib*. The parody which results from this is unusual; it depends less on a detailed relation of caricature between the imitation and the model, than on a relation of incongruity between it and common nature, and less on the mimicry of stylistic mannerisms (e.g. the archaisms and formulae which spatter his discourse in the early chapters), than on the extrapolation from chivalry books of principles of conduct. These he warps by his arrogance and dogmatism, embroiders in an idiosyncratic rationale, and expresses in a style which, in the imitative sense, is freely eclectic and creates a general effect of fulsomeness, pomposity, or bombast or, alternatively, of over-familiarity or even vulgarity. In most of the adventures we see Don Quixote re-enacting stereotyped situations rather than particular ones; this accords with Cervantes's withering disparagement of the genre as an undifferentiated plethora of types: 'that infinity of Amadises, that multitude of famous knights, so many emperors of Trebizond, Felixmartes of Hircania, palfreys, errant damsels. . .' (I, 49; i, 577). In most adventures considered so far, the stereotype serves merely as premise or starting-point of the re-enactment. Though the narrator's presentation of the phenomena and the hero's initial assumptions and responses may be moulded quite closely by it, the sequel, consisting in the spontaneous interplay between him and his circumstances, imitates it freely and indirectly. The same freedom of burlesque method is shown in the hoaxes played on the hero by clever characters or in the farcical mishaps and predicaments that Cervantes visits on him. They tend to consist less in the debased transposition of chivalresque adventures – e.g. the battle with the Basque (I, 8–9), the flight on Clavileño (II, 41) – than in the adaptation of familiar comic situations in the picaresque novel, the novella-tradition, the comic theatre. The hero's set-piece stories, descriptions, or speeches in chivalresque style show a greater degree of imitativeness, but this too, as we shall see, is highly eclectic.

Even adventures which seem to be based on specific incidents in chivalry books display these features. After the battle with the Basque, Don Quixote discovers with dismay that his flimsy, improvised helmet has been shattered and swears a mighty oath, in imitation of one sworn by the Marquis of Mantua in a famous old ballad, 'not to eat bread on linen cloth, nor dally with his wife, and other things which, though they now slip my memory, I take as read, until exacting thorough vengeance on him who did me this wrong' (I, 10; i, 150). The casual manner of reference to these abstemious conditions hardly measures up to the oath's intended solemnity; and things have indeed slipped the hero's – or Cervantes's – memory, since the conditions, as stipulated, occur in a different ballad. Sancho puts a reasonable objection to the intended revenge, and Don Quixote amends the oath, not in respect of the conditions, but the objective: capturing a helmet as good as the one broken. He adds: 'for I surely have someone to imitate in this, for the very same thing, to the letter, occurred over the helmet of Mambrino, which cost Sacripante so dear'. How could one be more punctilious? Yet the allusion to Sacripante is as casual and inexact as the reference to the ballad; and none of the contexts invoked belongs precisely to the chivalry books which supposedly inspire his thoughts, words, and deeds. Perhaps Don Quixote is confusing Sacripante with King Mambrino (if he was thinking of Boiardo's *Orlando Innamorato* I, iv, 81) or perhaps with Dardinel (see Ariosto's *Orlando Furioso* xviii, 151), or more probably with Ferrau, who vowed to capture the helmet that Orlando won from King Almonte (*Orlando Furioso* i, 29–31). In any case, when the helmet of Mambrino materialises (*DQ* I, 21), we are not required to recollect any context in particular, since none in particular is imitated. The circumstances imagined by Don Quixote correspond vaguely to several of those fleeting, sometimes hallucinatory encounters between pursuers and pursued that the Italian poets describe. Yet our attention is chiefly fixed on the altercation between master and squire as to the nature of the enigmatic object, and this has no 'source' other than the high/low dialectic of their relationship, and the particular stage that it has reached.

The altercation hums amusingly with acrimonious undertones of the disillusioning discovery of the fulling mills in the previous chapter. As he rides away from the melancholy scene of that incident, the hero, over-eager to recover lost face, announces with qualified confidence that he can descry a man coming towards them with the helmet of Mambrino on his head. He rashly draws the moral before the event with a little homily on the proverb: 'Where one door shuts, another opens.' Sancho, wary after the chastisement and reprimand which met his mirth upon that discovery, expresses scepticism with sly innuendo: *if* he could talk as freely as before, he *might* adduce reasons which might cause Don Quixote to recognise his error. Naturally, the innuendo goads his master to pass from qualified confidence to irate certainty (I, 21; i, 253):

'How can I be wrong in what I'm saying, you quibbling traitor . . . Tell me, don't you see that knight coming towards us, on a dapple grey horse, wearing a golden helmet on his head?'.
'All that I can see and make out', answered Sancho, 'is a man on an ass, grey like mine, wearing something that gleams on his head.'

The authority, exasperation, and lofty tone of the question are absurdly punctured by the reply: wary, laconic, and factual, and matching it point by point. The irony is enhanced by Cervantes's psychological finesse and made possible by his neutrality. So far he has not revealed what the object is; Sancho's wariness points to an outcome that common sense expects, but must, as yet, infer.

As Don Quixote prepares to charge, Cervantes furnishes the deliberately delayed, humdrum explanation: the man is a barber who has put his basin on his head to cover a new hat from a shower of rain. Terrified by Don Quixote's approach, he flees, leaving the spoils to the victor. The previous altercation is now renewed with a different tone and resolution. Sancho laughs to hear the thing referred to as a helmet, but remembering the recent consequences of similar mirth prudently offers an explanation for his laughter which meets Don Quixote half-way: 'It's funny to think what a big head the pagan who owned this helmet must have had; it looks just like a barber's basin.' Don Quixote, perhaps mollified by this moderation, perhaps magnanimous after victory, perhaps remembering his own mistake about the fulling mills, comes up with his first acknowledgement that the prosaic aspect of marvellous things is no insignificant accident to be casually brushed aside, but a permanent aspect which requires explanation. The one that he offers is deliciously barmy: the helmet must have fallen into the hands of an ignoramus who did not realise its true worth, and seeing it to be of pure gold, melted down the lower half for the money, turning the upper half into 'this, which looks like a basin, as you say'. It is another significant turning point in Don Quixote's evolution, portrayed with exquisite humour and finesse. But is it parody? Surely. Don Quixote's imitation of chivalry books consists, primordially, in trying to make a bridge between their fabulous world and the everyday one: he does this on the level of names and etymologies, of visual perceptions, of acts, and, as here, of ratiocination. This is all a continuous process. *Pace* Fielding, it is none the less parody for involving the lifelike study of character.

Don Quixote's attitude to the helmet soon incorporates his 'theory of relativity', according to which it is the lot of knights-errant to be persecuted by enchanters who keep turning appearances topsy-turvy, 'and so, what looks like a barber's basin to you looks like the helmet of Mambrino to me and will appear something different to someone else' (I, 25; i, 307). This is an essential part of the edifice of his evolving rationale, which also comprises a theory of history and chivalry's mission in it, of the knight-errant's cultural attainments, his diet, his amatory ethos, his social obligations, privileges, and exemptions. It is an extraordinary jumble of edifying maxims and fantastic rules, expounded with stylish aplomb; a good example of it is his explanation in II, 18 of how and why knight-errantry is an academic discipline which comprehends all others (jurisprudence, theology, knowledge of herbs, astrology, mathematics) and all the theological and cardinal virtues too.

The epithet *ingenioso* in the novel's title and Cervantes's description of his brainchild (the hero) as 'dry, wizened, capricious and full of diverse notions never imagined by anyone else' (prologue to Part I) indicate in advance what kind of improvisation we have to do with. Rabelais's Panurge and Sterne's Uncle Toby can prove anything under the sun with the aid of scholastic ratiocination and the citation of authorities. Don Quixote has rather similar accomplishments, except that he is not just engaged in proving a case, but acting a part, and his equipment includes humanistic eloquence and its related topics, and more generally, the magpie-like store of bookish knowledge proper to a compulsive reader.

His ability to embroider his imitation of chivalry with echoes of any style tonally adjacent to the romances and of any erudite matter thematically associable with them is well exemplified by his conversation with Sancho regarding his projected penance in the *sierra* (I, 25). He justifies his resolve with a rhetorically shaped, learned, and elegant exposition of the Renaissance doctrine of imitation. The major premise is: when one wants to reach the summit in any activity one must imitate its supreme practitioners; and this is amplified and proved with examples from painting, Homer, and Virgil. The first minor premise is: Amadís was the supreme knight-errant, and those of us who campaign beneath the banner of love and chivalry must imitate him; and the second is: one of the acts in which he showed most chivalric worth was his penance on the Peña Pobre, after he had been disdained by his lady Oriana. This elaborate syllogism, known to rhetoricians as *ratiocinatio*, is mounted like a wedding cake, with amplification, reduplication, periodic length and symmetry, syllabic cadences – the works. Soon Don Quixote adds, with elegant enumeration of circumstances, the examples of Orlando's acts of despair on discovering the signs of Angelica's affair with Medoro. The whole argument collapses absurdly, in the reader's eyes at least, with Sancho's objection: 'It seems to me that the knights who did thus were provoked and had cause for committing these follies and penances; but as for you, what cause have you for going mad?' (i, 305). Yet Don Quixote finds a crazily ingenious reply to this: 'That's just the point and subtlety of my enterprise. What thanks are due to a knight who goes mad *with* cause? The nub consists in going mad without one and giving my lady to understand that if I can do this when dry, what would I do when wet?' This, for the rhetoricians, is a strong type of argument: admission of the fact coupled with the assertion that it is not prejudicial to one's case but favourable. Shortly afterwards, Don Quixote performs his first penitential act, apostrophising the woodland deities in words which echo those of Albanio in Garcilaso's second eclogue. That done, he turns Rocinante loose with an exclamation echoing a commonplace conceit of lyric love poetry: 'I give thee liberty, I, who have it not' (i, 308); and ponders his steed's fleetness by comparison with two featured in *Orlando Furioso*. Challenged by Sancho as to the sense of behaving towards a mere country wench, Aldonza Lorenzo, as though she were a princess, he justifies his choice of her: (a) with the merry widow's saucy reason for choosing a lusty novice as her lover: 'For my purposes, he knows as much philosophy as Aristotle, and more'; (b) with the example of the poets who, in order to have matter for their verse and to pass themselves off as persons of spirit and feeling, invent mistresses for themselves with fancy names like Amaryllis, Phyllis, Sylvia; and (c) with the argument that since beauty and virtue are the essential movers of true love, Aldonza's low rank is a minor matter. This *sententia* would be a noble basis of argument if it were not simultaneously accompanied by the admission that the beauty and virtue are invented and elsewhere contradicted by the assertion that Dulcinea must be of high rank, since it is essential for a knight's lady to be so. Having settled Sancho's doubts, his master proceeds to draft two letters for him to deliver: one a tortuously convoluted entreaty to Dulcinea, evocative of the excesses of chivalric novelists like Feliciano de Silva; the other, ludicrously juxtaposed, a notarially and commercially worded letter of credit to his niece, authorising the gift of three donkey foals to Sancho. The virtuoso switching amongst registers, allusions, and frames of reference is breathtaking as well as being ridiculous by virtue of its cause.

To associate the ridiculous with the beautiful goes against the grain of classical aesthetics; yet this is what Cervantes asks us to do, at least in the stylistic domain. Rounding off his argument with the Canon of Toledo about the value of chivalry books, the hero exemplifies their delights with his improvised story of the knight of the lake (I, 50). It begins with an unmistakeable imitation of a typical situation in them: the description of a lake of seething pitch, full of serpents, from which issues a doleful voice inviting the knight to visit the seven fairy castles in its depths. This expands into an exuberantly lyrical pastiche of the descriptions of the Bowers of Bliss or enchanted palaces that are to be found in Italian heroic romances and Spanish pastoral romances: Elysian fields; a forest filled with the song of tiny, infinite, coloured birds; a brook whose fresh waters, like liquid crystal, run over tiny grains of sand and white pebbles like sifted gold and pure pearls; here a fountain of variegated jade; there a rustic grotto where shells of tiny cockles and twisted snails and pieces of gleaming crystal and imitation emerald are scattered with careless art; suddenly, over there, a castle which, despite being made of diamonds, carbuncles, rubies, pearls, gold and emeralds is more estimable in the design than the material. Precedents for this whimsical Baroque luxuriance are not to be found in chivalry books, crude and primitive by comparison. Rather, they lie in Tasso's *Gerusalemme liberata*, Lope de Vega's *La Arcadia*, Cervantes's own *Persiles*. The passage returns to a more recognisably chivalric path with the description of the group of damsels who lead the knight into the castle's interior, disrobe him, bathe him, anoint and robe him. Don Quixote's enthusiastic relish for what he describes is marked by a torrent of rhetorical questions, inviting awe (i, 585): 'Is it not a marvellous sight when, after all this, according to the story, he is led into another room to find the tables set with such propriety that he is left in awestruck wonderment? Isn't it marvellous to see him pouring on his hands water distilled of amber and fragrant flowers? And then to see him being made to sit on an ivory chair? And then being served by the damsels, all keeping a marvellous silence?' And so the hero proceeds, ending with the prosaic vision of the knight reclining in his chair after the meal, picking his teeth. The passage, by virtue of its premises, requires to be read as parody – parody of chivalry books. Yet as the Canon of Toledo's subsequent reactions testify (I, 50), Cervantes's purpose in writing it is also to characterise the eccentricity of this compulsive reader for whom reading *is* seeing and believing, and the crazily inventive wit which generates such well-concerted nonsense (*concertados disparates*), such exuberant flights of fancy, such widely nourished elegance.

The continual broadening of parody's scope seems to be accompanied by softening of its sting. The ambivalent mix of beauty and absurdity in the above-mentioned passage is typical of Cervantine parody in the high style: examples of it abound in the hero's discourse and the narrator's. The ambivalence may be traced to mixed motives in Cervantes: a frustrated poet-in-prose whose flights of fantasy or lyricism in his serious works are often curbed by puritanical scruples. He, or his characters for him, continually ask: Is this plausible? Is it excessive? Don Quixote's madness give his creator license to indulge his naughty penchant with a clear conscience, appeasing the puritan in him with the thought: all is well, I'm only joking. And indeed, he *is* only joking, despite the considerable similarities between Don Quixote's ravishing *locus amoenus* in I, 50 and the landscape descriptions in *La Galatea* Book VI and *Persiles* II, 15. The suggestion of rapt credulity in Don Quixote's description, its extravagant nonsense, and its lapse into prosaic banality with the mention of the toothpick reveal a controlling comic purpose. Cervantes's indulgence for his hero's *ingenio* stops well short of total identification, let alone identification with his chivalric mission.

Freely improvised, Don Quixote's character is in many ways an exaggeration or misapplication of romantic and heroic traits of a general kind rather than of chivalric traits in particular. A classic essay by José Montesinos of 1925 includes, in a discussion of the humorous servants of Lope de Vega's theatre, a characterisation of their masters; it is no coincidence that much of this stereotype seems tailor-made for Don Quixote. He also shares numerous affinities with the hero of Cervantes's Byzantine romance, *Persiles*: compassion for victims of persecution, prudish chastity, didactic sententiousness, a tourist's curiosity, inventive fantasy, and more besides. Hence there is often a disconcerting continuity between Don Quixote's mad behaviour and its exemplary counterparts. The stylishness of the exaggeration blurs its indecorum for us; the residual good sense and good intentions leave us uncertain how far, or even whether, it is aberrant, and where to draw the line between this residual lucidity and the real wisdom of his 'lucid intervals'. Add to these factors Cervantes's non-committal empathy, the subtlety and pervasiveness of his irony, and historical changes in the attitude to alienation – particularly in its literary representation, and the result is the notorious ambiguity that *Don Quixote* holds for modern readers. Cervantes, who describes his book as 'so clear that there is nothing with which to find difficulty in it' (II, 3; ii, 64), would no doubt have been utterly mystified by this response. For him, what differentiates exaggerated or misapplied heroics from the real thing is always the principle of decorum; he often does not trouble to signal it because he takes the intuition of it for granted. For ambiguity, read tone-deafness.

The Sanchification of Panza

Within the relative framework of 'plus ça change . . .' Sancho undergoes a moral transformation in Part II, which Madariaga (1961) defined in the phrase 'the Quixotification of Sancho'. My own amendment of this formula would go thus: the Quixot-ification and Teresification of Sancho and the Sanchification of Panza. The process of change is determined by fugal repetition, that is, the transference of traits and themes from one character to another in a way that is partly independent of influence.

A passage of conversation in I, 21 typifies the as yet unregener-ate Panza of Part I, encouraged in this condition by his master. It follows Don Quixote's imaginary sketch of the career of 'the Knight of the Sun' designed to explain for his squire's benefit the circumstances in which he may expect to receive his just reward. The story, implicitly a projection of Don Quixote's own *curriculum vitae*, culminates in the knight's marriage by hook or by crook to an *infanta*, followed by acquisition of her father's king-dom. 'And what of Dulcinea?' is the question pertinently asked in a footnote by the great nineteenth-century editor of *Don Quixote*, Diego Clemencín. Sancho wonders what will accrue to the poor squire prior to the enthronement. Perhaps he will have to be content with marriage to the *infanta's* damsel-in-waiting. 'And what of Señora Panza?', one might ask. The conversation proceeds thus (i, 263):

'Who's to prevent it [marriage to the damsel]?', said Don Quixote.
'In that case', answered Sancho, 'we need only trust in God and let fortune run as he best directs.'
'Let him provide', replied Don Quixote, 'according to my desire and your need, and worse luck to the man with a low opinion of himself.'
'Amen', said Sancho, 'for I'm an old Christian [quasi-proverbial expression: 'yo cristiano viejo soy'], and that's good enough for me to be a count.'
'More than enough', said Don Quixote, 'and even if you weren't, it wouldn't signify, because once I'm king, I can easily ennoble you, with-out your needing to buy the title or render me any service. Because once you're a count, lo and behold you're a knight [colloquialism: 'cátate ahí

caballero'], and let them say what they please. My word, they'll call you my lord, like it or not.'

'You bet [plebeian ejaculation: '¡montas que!'] I'd carry the tittle [solecism of *lictado* for *dictado*] with dignity!', said Sancho.

'Title, not tittle', said his master.

'Very well', replied Sancho. 'I tell you it would look fine on me, because strike me dead if I wasn't once convenor of a religious brotherhood, and I looked so fine in a convenor's robes that they all said I had the presence to be a senior brother. If that's so, won't I look a swell with a duke's robes on, or dressed in gold and pearls like a foreign count? I reckon people from a hundred leagues around will come to see me.'

'You'll look very well', said Don Quixote, 'but you'll need to get your beard cut often; it's so thick, tangled, and unkempt that if you don't trim it every two days at least, people will see you for what you are a gunshot away.'

The proverbial folly of counting chickens or eating pie-in-the-sky is the subject of two famous Spanish farces of the mid-sixteenth century, and the conversations on the theme of the governorship in Part I indirectly but unmistakably echo them. The passage cited above plays on another comic motif associated with this theme. A character in a play by Tirso de Molina, thinking of a peasant dressed in court finery, describes him as 'a wall of adobe brick covered in silk carpeting'. Clothes may be taken as a metonymy for all the attributes of high status. By making the characters dwell with such homely particularity on the minutiae of Sancho's dizzy elevation, Cervantes highlights its ludicrous unfittingness. The familiar tone is not just struck by Sancho's plebeian register and reference to village festivals but by his master's discourse: 'cátate ahí caballero' and the mundane talk of shaving are *not* language appropriate to Amadís. One also perceives, between the lines of the passage, mild satire at *parvenu* nobility. Above all it exemplifies the innocent opportunism and highhandedness of the conversations on the governorship in Part I, particularly on Sancho's side. Sancho's remark about being of old Christian stock (i.e. not descended from Jewish or Moorish ancestors) is the seed of his whole future development, positive as well as negative. To the barber, chiding him for his foolish ambitions, he declares stoutly in I, 47: 'though poor, I'm an old Christian; and I owe nothing to anyone; and if I want islands others want worse, and deeds make the man; and being a man I can come to be Pope' (i, 563). Here is a characteristic string of proverbs or adapted proverbs on the theme 'I'm as good as the next man, since all are basically equal'. The foolish peasants of Cervantes's comic theatre have the same mentality: a fatuous sense of their own merit and right to the perquisites, but not the obligations, of responsible office, merely on the strength of their pure blood.

These declarations have a sententious quality thanks to their proverbial nature, and thus contain potential for development along more edifying lines than those just considered. We first observe glimmerings of the future governor's wisdom in a speech where Sancho considers the possibility of *not* getting the governorship. To Sansón Carrasco he says (II, 4):

And if he [Don Quixote] weren't to give me an island, God will provide [proverbial: 'nacido soy', meaning literally 'I'm born']; and a man should put his trust in none but his maker; and perhaps ungoverned bread ['pan desgobernado'] will taste just as good as the bread that I eat as governor, if not better; and who knows if the devil isn't lying in wait to trip me up with one of those governorships, so that I stumble and fall and knock out my teeth. (ii, 71)

He will develop these themes at greater length in conversations with the Duchess (II, 33) and his master (II, 43) when the governorship is imminent. With proverbs, as with statistics, one can argue anything. From the core idea of men's spiritual and physical equality, Sancho arrives at a position opposite to that of the frivolous opportunism of Part I. Even *he* communes in the mood of morally earnest *desengaño* typical of Cervantes in his late years and, more generally, of the epoch. Yet he does so lightly, earthily, and comically with talk of 'pan desgobernado' (the untranslatable pun plays with the normal sense of 'desgobernar', meaning to turn topsy turvy, and also with the proverb 'tan buen pan hacen aquí como en Francia', meaning 'they make as good bread here as in France') and knocking out teeth. More-over, at this stage his wisdom is merely vestigial. The speech in II, 4 ends with a more characteristic thought: 'but if . . . without too much effort or risk heaven should send me an island or simi-lar, I wouldn't be such a fool as to turn it down'. Naturally, he finds apt proverbs for it: 'Cuando te dieren la vaquilla, corre con la soguilla' ('When they give you the cow, come quick with the halter') and 'Cuando viene el bien, métalo en tu casa' ('when good luck comes your way, take it home and put it there').

Fugal motifs, in the examples just considered, are repeated with greater or lesser variation by the same person. Now let us consider a case in which motifs are transferred. Of his wife Teresa, Sancho ruefully says that there is no mallet that can apply such pressure to the hoops of a barrel as she can apply to a person to bend him to her will (II, 7). Evidence of this capacity is provided by her conversation with her husband in II, 5 and its long-term effects on him. During it, the 'translator' keeps advert-ing to Sancho's implausibly elevated style, and thus incidentally draws attention to his imitation of his master's authoritativeness; yet it is Teresa who really wears the trousers. Sancho, back in his familiar role of counting chickens, is here chiefly concerned with the advancement of his wife and daughter. Teresa opposes him with the very proverbial wisdom about contentment with one's lot that he articulated in the previous chapter, and with a typically Sanchpanzine stylistic repertoire: proverbs, solecisms, pictur-esque epithets, rustic analogues: 'Let the chicken live, even though it has the pip', she declares (ii, 74). She echoes Job's pious resignation: 'Naked came I from my mother's womb. . .' (Job I, 21); so, elsewhere, does her husband (see p. 56). She says that the world's best sauce is hunger, and since the poor never lack it they always eat with relish; thematically, this is akin to Sancho's thought about 'ungoverned bread' tasting as good as the 'gov-erned' variety. Yet, fugally repetitive even in this, she is led by wifely and motherly opportunism to qualify the foregoing good sense with: 'But look, Sancho: if by chance you should land up with some governorship, don't forget me and your children.'

This prompts Sancho to talk of marrying Mari-Sancha so high that they will have to call her my lady: fugal repetition of what his master said to *him* in I, 21. To this his wife replies (ii, 75): 'Not that, Sancho . . . marry her with her kind, that's the best. If you take her out of clogs and put her in lady's high soled shoes and out of plain brown frocks into farthingales and silk slit skirts and from Marykins and thou to *Doña* So-and-So and My Lady, the girl won't know where she is and will put her foot in it at every turn, showing the true stitching of her coarse cloth.' Fugal repetition again: of Sancho's visions of himself dressed in ducal robes and his master's premonitions of his tell-tale shaggy beard. Soon, illustrating the proverb: 'Wipe the nose of the boy next door and set him up in your own house', she conjures counter-prospects of Mari-Sancha married to strapping Lope Tocho and blessing their old age with a brood of children and in-laws. Nor is she tempted by the thought of being styled Doña Teresa Panza and sitting amongst cushions in the best pews in church, in defiance of the gossip of the gentlewomen (ii, 76): 'I was always one for equality, brother, and I can't stand people putting on airs without a right. They called me Teresa at baptism, a plain unvarnished name, without additions, frills, or trimmings of *dones* or *donas*.' Here she gives a radical twist to her husband's preoccupation with the equality of men; she also echoes his habit of coining paired synonyms in which one term is the barbarous masculine or feminine of the other: a motif associated with Sancho's references to the governorship (Rosenblat [1971], p. 176).

The impression of Teresa's mallet (see p. 74) becomes evident many chapters later, just prior to and during Sancho's governorship, particularly in his abdication speech. Yet the relative moral stature that he will later assume derives not only from Teresa's brand of self-interested caution, summed up in 'Mind your place', but also from Don Quixote's superior wisdom, particularly the second precept of his counsels of government: 'Know thyself' (II, 42). Sancho's performance in office is obviously in some sense a fulfilment of those counsels. And his reiterated preference of the soul's welfare to the corrupting effects of climbing the greasy pole (II, 4, 33, 43) accords with a dominant, and eventually the prevailing, preoccupation of his master in Part II. So Quixot-ification is an important factor in Sancho's development too. As he would put it (e.g. II, 10; ii, 106): 'No con quien naces, sino con quien paces' (roughly, 'nurture not nature'). Yet even more important than the factors mentioned is the actualisation of the wise potential latent in his loyalty, decency, commonsense, and proverbial lore, conceived as essentially rustic qualities. Hence my phrase about the Sanchification of Panza: that is, the refine-ment of crude rusticity ('panza' means belly) by the possibilities enshrined in the proverb 'They call virtuous silence Sancho'. This might seem a natural process: an eliciting of virtues contained in Sancho's individual or ancestral psyche. Yet to a greater extent it is a spectacular example of 'functional transference'.

Had Cervantes made Sancho, as governor, conform to predict-able stereotype, the result would have been equivalent to the nitwitted mayors of his and his epoch's comic theatre. One of his farces, concerning the election to the office of mayor in a small village, gives a clue as to why he did not go down this path. The first three candidates are as frivolous in their pretensions as the Sancho of Part I. The fourth is made of worthier stuff: honest, well-intentioned, and conscious of his place in the social hier-archy. He chides an insubordinate sacristan with this forelock-tugging sentiment, repeated by Cervantes on other occasions: 'Leave those in authority over us alone, for they know their obli-gations better than we do; if they are bad, pray for their reform; if good, for their preservation.' Sancho exhibits the same virtues on a grander scale. His supreme act of wisdom consists in resign-ing: i.e. knowing his place. Despite his previous fantasies of unchecked lotus eating and nest feathering, he leaves the governorship with empty pockets and an exhausting, conscien-tiously fulfilled schedule of administration behind him. Cervantes has a typically Spanish suspicion of the intricacies and corruption of the law and of government, particularly town-hall government. His ideal of the good judge or governor is reflected in Sancho's straight-from-the-hip, commonsensical, equitable settlement of cases and his zealous stamping out of vagabondage and racketer-ring. This is an anti-Machiavellian, simplistic, and conservative ideal, which puts a premium on integrity and reflects the age's concept of kingship as a pastoral Christ-like tutelage. Don Quix-ote's precepts, with their ethical and non-political bias, express it clearly. Thus, Cervantes took the subject of government too seriously to treat Sancho's tenure of office in a merely frivolous way. This seriousness is reflected in his sporadic, unexpected displays of moral maturity when the governorship is imminent and in the authority, gravity, and worldly wisdom that he miracu-lously assumes when he takes up office and to some extent relin-quishes with it. A farcical style of treatment would also have been out of keeping with the morally reflective nature of *Don Quixote* Part II. Yet the novel's light tone, the risible nature of Sancho and, above all, Cervantes's natural reticence about political mat-ters inevitably channel the expression of these ideals of govern-ment in an oblique and inoffensive form, which blends serious-ness with farce, fantasy, and legend.

Sancho's achievement of his seemingly impossible ambition brings this major theme to a perfect and astonishing culmination: astonishing, amongst other reasons, because Sancho belies every-body's expectation that he will make a ridiculous hash of the job. True, he is ingenuously unaware that the 'island' that the Duke has bestowed on him is really a town somewhere in Aragon, that he is a puppet governor manipulated by his underlings, the Duke's servants, and that some of the cases submitted to him are contrived tests or practical jokes. Aristocrats in this age often had fun with their jesters in this way: letting them masquerade as dignitaries ot take part in tourneys. Sancho's governorship, and the *burlas* in the Duke's palace in general, are obviously influenced by these burlesque court charades. His tormentor-in-chief is the *opera bufa* figure of Dr Pedro Recio Tirteafuera, related not just to the pedants and doctors of the comic stage but also to the miserly tutors of the picaresque novel, always ready with pious sophisms about the benefits of a starvation diet to body and soul. Yet 'he stood up to them all, though foolish, coarse and fat' (preamble to II, 49).

The factors that Cervantes half-jokingly adduces to explain the prodigy – his master's precepts, the stimulus of office, divine inspiration, Sancho's innate potential – hardly suffice to render realistic the transformation of ignorant, jocose, greedy Sancho into a paragon of judicial wisdom. Cervantes hints by his manner of presentation that the transformation belongs to fantasy, not real life. The cases brought for Sancho's adjudication include traditional riddles and riddle-like jests (II, 45 and 51), a marriage-suit which is mainly a pretext for the burlesque portrait of the prospective bride (II, 47), the romantic story of a teenage esca-pade (II, 49) – i.e. hardly ones which might exercise a magistrate in real life. The two which most nearly merit the name – the judgement of the gold coins in the staff and of the false accusation of rape (II, 45) – are based on devotional literature; both cast Sancho in a role defined by the medieval *exemplum* tradition: the wise judge who, by his acumen, saves an innocent man from being wronged by a clever fraud. Yet, though Cervantes taps these fictitious sources, he makes the prodigy look possible. How?

Partly he does this by maintaining a realistic balance between Sancho's intrinsic comicality and his new-found *gravitas*. This gives depth and a certain ambivalence to the comedy. The mock-assault on the 'island' (II, 53) is designed by the perpetrators to precipitate Sancho's departure. They achieve their end, yet the manner of his leaving makes a dignified contrast with their provo-cation of it. Cervantes should not be credited with moral super-iority here. His description of how the alarm is sounded in the town at dead of night with bells, shouting, trumpets, and drums builds up an impressive atmosphere of crisis and is meant to arouse our wonderment. The mood changes to hilarity with the description of how the governor, strapped in his monstrous cara-pace of armour, is humiliatingly trampled underfoot. The relish with which Cervantes switches his vivid and degrading analogies suggests that he shares the merrymakers' glee; and his allusions to Sancho's terror underline the joke's efficacy rather than invite compassion:

> There he was like a turtle enclosed and covered by its shell, or like a half side of ham pressed between two tubs, or just like a boat keeled over on the sand; and not a scrap of pity did the sight of his fallen body cause those merry persons. Rather, extinguishing their torches, they renewed their cries more loudly, urgently reiterating 'To arms!' and passing over his body, with numberless stabs upon those shields, so much so that if he had not huddled and shrunk and tucked his head between them it would have gone badly for the poor governor.   (ii, 442)

Pity is latent in the ending, and it emerges patently in the sequel which, without forsaking humour, does justice to the gravity of Sancho's decision to quit. The burlesque euphoria of the pranksters' acclaim for his valour contrasts with his dignified rejection of it: 'Enemies I've conquered? My eye! I'm not interested in sharing out spoils, just in asking some friend, if I have one, to give me a drop of wine, because I'm parched, and wipe off this sweat, because I'm dripping.' The description of his subsequent actions, reflecting his inward resolve, have a sober and factual simplicity. This, together with the awed curiosity of the bystanders, enhances their significance: 'They wiped him, brought him the wine, undid his shields and he sat on his bed and fainted from the fear, the shock, and the fatigue . . . He asked what time it was, and they answered that it was already dawn. He fell silent and, saying no more, began to dress, buried in silence, with everybody looking at him and wondering what was the purpose of his dressing so fast.' Then he goes to the stable, embraces and kisses his ass, and tearfully addresses to him – symbol of the homely things that he forsook to become governor – the preamble of his abdication speech. Pathos verging on sentimentality mingles with comedy here. Yet the bad taste, if such it is, is redeemed by the speech itself, an impressive expression of pent-up disillusionment and mature resolve (ii, 444): 'Make way, sirs, and let me return to my former liberty; let me return to my former life so that I may be resurrected from this present death. I wasn't born to be governor, nor to defend islands or cities from their attackers. I know more about ploughing and digging, pruning vines and trussing them, than about making laws or defending provinces and kingdoms.' Don Quixote too, on leaving the Duke's palace, will contrast, with heartfelt relief, the possibility of enjoying a crust of bread in freedom with the servitude of being indebted for *haute cuisine* to a lordly patron. Cervantes treats both departures as recoveries of liberty, physical as well as moral: an experience fraught for him with emotional significance. Yet Sancho's speech is humorously in character: though it turns on the time-honoured topics of Country *versus* Court, it is no pale echo of Virgil's *Georgics*. He employs examples, analogies, colloquialisms, and proverbs bristling with peasant stubbornness and no-nonsense directness, reminiscent of Teresa's style and temper: 'I'd rather stuff myself with *gazpachos* than be subject to the meanness of an impertinent doctor who starves me to death'; 'I'm one of the Panzas, who are all stubborn, and, for them, once it's nay it's nay, even though it be yea, no matter what anyone else may think.' He echoes Teresa's contrasts between court finery or footwear and the homespun alternative: 'Let's tread level ground once more; if my feet aren't adorned with fancy Cordoba leather, they won't lack for hemp *alpargatas*.' The punch line of his rejoinder to Dr Pedro Recio is superb: 'Each sheep with its mate, and don't stick your leg out further than the sheet allows, and let me pass, for it's getting late.' It is one of the great scenes of the novel, and Sancho's finest hour.

Its memorability is due, amongst other factors, to Cervantes's peculiar knack of seamless and unobtrusive 'quotation'. The traditional precedents of Sancho's wisdom in the governorship, apart from the ones already mentioned, include the mystique attaching to the figure of the fool, legendary exempla of peasants (e.g. the Visigothic king Wamba) who acquit themselves well as rulers, the wise rustics of Lope de Vega's theatre who prefer their simple lot to the cares of court, various Renaissance Utopias or portraits of the ideal prince, the burlesque enthronements of Carnival (Redondo, 1978). And implicit in the episode as a whole is a network of critical or reformist ideas about justice, government, and the requisites of honour and social advancement. *Implicit* is the key-word. For Coleridge the difference between allegory and symbol, and the reason for the latter's power of implication, lies in its embodiment of the universal in the particular. Sancho's governorship – and, more generally, his and his master's character – are eminently 'symbolic' in this sense.

Paradoxes of Part II; Quixote's disillusionment

The paradoxes mentioned above concern the hero's morale and society's and the reader's response to it; partly, they are objectively 'there' in the text, yet to an even greater extent they are caused by the modern reader's propensity to sentimentalise and idealise the hero's character.

Part II has a celebratory purpose, which affects its nature in various ways, some already noted (see pp. 44–5). The atmosphere is more serene and harmonious than Part I's rumbustiousness; the pageant staged by the city of Barcelona, and lyrically described in II, 61, sums it up. Preceded by a letter from Roque Guinart to one of his friends in Barcelona, Don Quixote and Sancho are guided to the city and are left outside it, on the beach, on Midsummer's Eve. In the letter Roque said that he wished that he could have reserved the entertainment of their company for his friends, the faction of the Niarros, denying it to his enemies, the Cadells, yet he feared that this was impossible, since the lunatic and discreet utterances of Don Quixote and the sallies of his squire could not fail to give pleasure universally (end of II, 60). The sight that greets the pair's eyes at dawn, as they behold the sea for the first time, represents Barcelona's homage to them – indeed, Nature's and the Spanish Navy's too. As Roque expected, joy is unconfined. White dawn shows her face at the balconies of the Orient, liveried horsemen sally from the city to the accompaniment of fifes and drums, galleys with streaming pennants execute manoeuvres on the placid waters, and their cannons fire salutes which are answered from the city walls. Cervantes summarises: 'The cheerful sea, the jocund earth, the clear air, smudged only by the artillery smoke, seemed to infuse sudden pleasure in everybody' (II, 61; ii, 507). The pageant's purpose is burlesque, as is evident from the salutation addressed to Don Quixote by one of the horsemen, yet also it is welcoming and theatrical.

'Recognition' is the indispensable prerequisite of 'celebration': many chapters (e.g. II, 3, 4, 7, 58, 59, 72) have little purpose beyond these two. The two heroes go through their paces, revealing their mannerisms, and society pays them its tribute with reactions that have already been described (see p. 45). The sense of being the very subjects of a published chronicle is a feeling gratifying to both, giving them a new self-consciousness and furnishing Don Quixote with concrete proof of having achieved his goal. His gratification reaches its zenith with his reception by the Duke and Duchess: literal realisation of the dream-synopsis of his future career that he improvised in I, 21. For modern readers, these protracted jests seem cruel precisely because of their mockingly detailed fulfilment of the two heroes' cherished illusions.

Because of that reception 'that was the first day when he [Don Quixote] wholly knew and believed himself to be a real knight errant and not a fantastic one' (ii, 274). This remark by Cervantes in II, 31 throws interesting retrospective light on the hero's psyche and is typical of the suggestive yet unanalytic way in which it is portrayed. The remark implies that his delusions have so far rested on a basis of repressed doubt. Of this there have indeed been occasional signs: e.g. evasions of inconvenient evidence, or revealing self-corrections, by which 'I think' or 'I imagine' becomes 'I know' (see p. 64). Yet the signs, strewn casually and incidentally, are easy to miss and lack definite implication. Furthermore, the remark implies that Don Quixite's doubt has been virtually dispelled at a stage when the signs of it have been mounting. And – a further paradox – these have been mounting when the grounds of reassurance have been getting stronger. For if the hero can gloat over real or imagined victories (II, 16 and 17) and bask in the simulated admiration of his readership (*passim*), why is he depicted as sporadically melancholy and dispirited (e.g. II, 44) and why does he show evident symptoms of waning delusion?

Since Cervantes provides no key with which to unlock these riddles of a vividly lifelike but insane psychology, it is tempting to call amateur modern psychology in aid. I prefer to explain them in terms more intelligible to him. We may begin by reducing the paradox's scope. For the Spanish Golden Age there was no contradiction between a sense of worldly triumph and one of disillusionment. Thus, after offering to render homage to the fair shepherdesses with a feat of arms on their behalf, and having been humiliatingly trampled by bulls for his pains, the hero gives vent to this: 'I, Sancho, was born to live dying and you to die eating . . . Consider me a subject of printed histories, famous in arms, courteous in my acts, respected by princes, solicited by damsels; and at the end of all, when I expected palms, triumphs, and crowns as the merited reward of my deeds, this morning I have found myself trampled, kicked, and pounded by the feet of vile, unclean animals – a consideration which blunts my teeth, dulls my molars, and numbs my hands and quite takes my appetite from me' (II, 59; ii, 482). He ponders this as a singular misfortune; yet the moral wisdom of the age insisted on the banality of such vicissitudes in the cosmic scheme. This moral meditation arises from the spectacle of Sancho finding solace in a snack and is rendered ridiculous by that circumstance: note the deliciously flat beginning and ending. It is a good example of the lightness and levity with which Cervantes treats Don Quixote's disillusionment in Part II.

Having reduced the paradox, we may explain it thus. The premises of Part II pull the hero in two different directions. The first of these is what may be called the process of his disillusionment. Cervantes emphasises the sporadic lucidity which was only a secondary aspect of his character in Part I, and also continues to show him adjusting his delusions to experience and being gradually chastened by it. Thus Cervantes prepares for his ultimate return to sanity, and begins the process from the beginning of his third sally. In Chaper 11, Don Quixote encounters an apparition which, like the fantasmagorical cortège in I, 19, seems really to herald an adventure: a cart driven by an ugly devil, bearing the figure of Death, an angel with painted wings, an emperor with a gold crown, and other marvellous personifications. He issues his customary challenge and receives the 'devil's' reasonable explanation of the prodigy: this is a company of actors travelling to a nearby locality to stage a religious play as part of the feast of Corpus Christi. His urbanely lucid reaction to this is pointedly different from what we have come to expect (see p. 43). Significant contrasts like this keep being forced upon us. His humility after having smashed up Master Peter's puppet show includes the recognition that enchanters have caused him to see mere puppets as chivalric characters (II, 26). This precisely reverses what he typically asserts in Part I (I, 8, 18, 25). His admission of failure after the adventure of the enchanted boat has an unprecedently defeatist ring: 'May God remedy it; the whole world consists of machines and designs contrary to each other. I can do no more' (II, 29; ii, 267). In view of the primordial significance in the novel of his delusions about inns, the fact that he does *not* see an inn as a castle in Chapter 24 is obviously striking. Much later, a similar occurrence elicits from the narrator the remark that after his defeat at Barcelona Don Quixote's wits generally improved (II, 71); this implies that defeats in general have had a chastening effect on him: no doubt the cause of his relative lucidity at an earlier stage. Immediately prior to his return to his village he gloomily interprets two trivial incidents as bad omens for his prospects of seeing Dulcinea again (II, 73). His frustration over the tardiness or the possibility of Dulcinea's disenchantment in late Part II is another source of chastening depression and an evident cause of his terminal illness.

This impression of a change for the better is strongly established in the first thirty chapters of Part II. No longer a mere object of derision or pity, the hero is now regarded by society – e.g. by Don Diego and his son (II, 16–18), the personages at Camacho's wedding (II, 19–22), the ex-page (II, 24) – as a learned and fascinating, if eccentric, *companion*. His passages of crazy sophistry show a slippery proximity to lucidity; Don Diego's son even complains of the difficulty of pinning his madness down (II, 18; ii, 172–73). The dives into blatant lunacy are less obdurate and aggressive than before: partly because they are often the result of other people's plausible trickery, rather than of rashly enacted, spontaneous misapprehensions; partly because they are qualified by doubt, bafflement, mild deference to the scepticism of others, even playful irony. The Cave of Montesinos story, central to his delusions in Part II, appears a self-indulgent, defensive retreat into a private fantasy-world. The Don's general demeanour – innocent trustfulness, liberality, peaceableness, disarming humility – justifies the epithet 'el bueno' that Cervantes bestows upon him at the end (II, 74; ii, 589).

Then, in Chapter 30, a seemingly anomalous shift of emphasis takes place. At this point the hero arrives at the country-seat of a Duke and Duchess in Aragon and stays there as an 'honoured' guest until Chapter 58. The treatment that these aristocrats mete out to him consists mainly of elaborately staged *burlas* designed to play up to his and Sancho's delusions, exploiting them as a source of communal entertainment; it continues in Barcelona, where he is the guest of another noble gentleman, Don Antonio Moreno (II, 60-65). Modern criticism has regarded this conversion of the two heroes into something like court fools with distaste; analogies have even been drawn between the merry victimisation of Don Quixote and Christ's Passion. The charge of insensitivity laid against the Duke and Duchess is partly understandable; it is supported by Cide Hamete's accusation against them of having carried the joke too far (II, 70; ii, 564-65). Supposedly paragons of civilised *savoir-faire*, they treat the hero with solicitude but little of the friendly equality and partial respect shown by previous acquaintances in Part II. Their primary aim, tirelessly pursued, is to extract as much amusement from him and Sancho as possible. Yet Don Antonio Moreno's aim is no different. The stress laid on his urbane sense of where to draw the line (beginning of II, 62) shows that Cervantes has no reservations about the principle on which the *burlas* are based, merely about the manner and degree of implementation. In any case, his eventual condemnation of the Duke and Duchess seems tainted by double standards; he blames the doer but relishes the deed. He would surely not have devoted so much space to these *burlas* – 'the best adventures that this great history contains' (end of II, 33) – had he not expected the reader to share and approve this relish. By putting the limelight on the burlesque artistry of the pranksters, and treating the victims as credulous foils, he diverts attention from the process of the hero's disillusionment, not putting him or it stage-centre once again until he gets him out of stately homes and on the open road.

The shift of emphasis involves no contradiction of the novel's premises. Part II is in a full sense a sequel to Part I, continuing and developing its major themes, including its burlesque theme, and celebrating the popularity of its two heroes, particularly as comic butts. This entails the vigorous survival of the core of Don Quixote's delusions, which change in their outward form – from extrovert dynamism to passive credulity – but do not collapse until the very end. It is concordant with Part II's celebratory nature that the initiative should pass from the hero to his fan-club, hence that the adventures should chiefly assume the pattern of the communally staged charade: sophisticated sequels to the practical jokes of Part I, enacted by readers intimate with its premises, and reminiscent of the festival pageants, the masques, and farces in which the principal figures of Part I often appeared in contemporary Spain. Thus, the *burlas* should not primarily be regarded as a symptom of the merry-makers' – and perhaps high society's – frivolity, but rather as the culminating tribute by the whole community of *Don Quixote*'s readers to its two protagonists' entertainment-value. As an act of homage made by *readers*, it is also an interpretation of where its entertainment-value essentially lies.

Modern readers, and more especially the critics, have felt Cervantes's shift of emphasis as involving a contradictory pull on their interest in the hero. Since Dr Johnson's time (see p. 57), they have tended to be more interested in what aligns Don Quixote with normal experience than what alienates him, and, so far as Part II is concerned, more in his process of disillusionment than in his risibility. Hence, in relation to what happens from Chapter 30 onwards, they have preferred to regard him as noble victim of an unfeeling society and to extend that perception to the whole of Part II. This is well illustrated by a common critical approach to his delusions about Dulcinea's enchantment, which are induced by Sancho's trickery in II, 10, and become thereafter Don Quixote's main preoccupation, and the basis for a principal sequence of *burlas* (II, 35, with numerous repercussions). The approach, deriving from Madariaga (1961, Chapters 7 ff.), is as follows. However absurd, Dulcinea is the hero's sustaining ideal; Sancho's fraud outside El Toboso delivers a shattering blow to it; his doubts surface subconsciously in the story of the Cave of Montesinos, where he sees Dulcinea in enchanted form and 'everywhere there is an atmosphere of psychological and physical decline. . .When ideals come to this, disillusion is pathetically sad and no longer funny' (Parker [1985], p. 115). This would suggest that the proper musical accompaniment to the theme of Dulcinea in Part II ought to be a thousand sobbing violins. Whence the discrepancy between the response just cited and that which the text not only invites but *depicts* in its readership? The typical argument that the depicted response, and the narrator's implied endorsement of it by his levity, are just so many 'viewpoints' that we can set aside, seems to me a facile evasion of the difficulty.

The reasons for the discrepancy have partly to do with posterity's reception of *Don Quixote* and with the cultural factors that conditioned it: powerfully and subliminally, they predispose the modern reader to interpret Cervantes's hero through the perspective of Western literature's re-creation of the Quixote-type (see Chapter 3). To put it simply, that literature's canonical texts have been teaching us for over two and half centuries to question the system of values presupposed by Cervantes: one which treats imaginative excess or individualistic truancy as being, ultimately, an offence to reasonable, socially acceptable norms of behaviour.

His undoubted artistic sympathy for the offence is firmly embedded in that premise; by contrast, our cultural conditioning prompts us to interpret the sympathy as having a more radical significance. To be sure, our expectations would scarcely get a purchase were it not for the ironies, ambiguities, and virtualities of meaning in Cervantes's novel that seem to encourage them.

The chief ambiguity concerns a nice, implicit act of discrimination that Cervantes expects from us. Don Quixote's chivalric enterprise constantly hovers on the border of ideals of heroism that Cervantes applauds (see p. 70), differing from them essentially in its literary, hence fabulous and anachronistic, form. That difference makes them irredeemably absurd for Cervantes. Not so for posterity. Since the nineteenth century, Cervantine criticism has traditionally made a distinction between the hero's noble ideals and absurd delusions; the dichotomy was formulated in classic lectures by Menéndez Pelayo (1905) and Menéndez Pidal (1920). Of the scores of comments on the hero's behaviour in the course of *Don Quixote*, not one – apart from claims by the hero himself – lends it support. To be sure, Cervantes gives credit to his goodness of character, but he goes no further than that. He could scarcely be expected to, in view of his insistence that his protagonist's crazy imitation of chivalry affects his *thoughts*, hence principles of action, as well as deeds and perceptions. His insistent opposition between Quixote's chimerical *caballería* and its authentic modern counterparts smothers in him any sense of the former's residual value. If he had this sense, he would surely not repeatedly juxtapose the two kinds of chivalry in order to show up the literary version as ridiculously ineffectual.

In the remainder of this chapter I propose to examine Don Quixote's attitude to Dulcinea, tracing its development as far as the Cave of Montesinos story. My general purpose in so doing is to correct the errors of perspective which lead us to regard the burlesque treatment of Don Quixote – not just by the practical jokers but also by Cervantes – as incongruous with his character: i.e. as being excessive and unmerited. My specific purposes are twofold. First, by examining how an important aspect of this character is built up, we can see that, despite its compelling aura of lifelikeness, it rests on a basis of arbitrary artificiality which attests the primordial role of burlesque in Cervantes's conception of it. This 'unreality', which affects Sancho too, is equivalent to fugal repetition and functional transference; it is to some extent camouflaged and justified by Quixote's madness and Sancho's simplemindedness. The interpretation that I propose is at odds with the dichotomy of ideals and delusions, which constantly relegates comedy to the externals of the hero's behaviour and rests on an excessively naturalistic conception of it. Thus, if we revert to Parker's above-cited remarks about the vision in the cave, we perceive the assumption that there is a seriously felt, consistent core in the hero's attitude to his mistress, as in normal human emotions or ideals. The seediness of the vision of Dulcinea is explained, in psychologically realistic terms, as the pathological symptoms of a spiritual breakdown; and the appropriate response to it is declared to be understanding pity, not mirth. For me, the seediness is consistent with a grotesque vein of comedy which envelops the theme of Dulcinea from the outset. It is manifest in the hero's mad – i.e. comically arbitrary – proneness to lapse from precious excess to banal vulgarity, and in the dislocation of his behaviour from normal motives: e.g. having some notion of his mistress as a real, individual person. All this elicits from Cervantes, quite logically, a nonchalant and detached focus on the hero's amatory feelings. Secondly, this comic grotesqueness has a moral significance. Cervantes habitually uses comedy – situational ironies, exaggerated traits – as an economical way of conveying a moral view of the conduct thus represented. Humour's exemplary code saves him from the aesthetic impropriety, as he sees it, of preaching. A primary reason why the sentimental idealisation of Don Quixote needs to be resisted is that it renders the code, hence the underlying sense of the novel, impenetrable.

Quixote and Dulcinea

From the beginning of the novel there seem to be two Dulcineas, the ideal in Don Quixote's mind and various rustic travesties outside it. This appearance is misleading: Dulcinea is really a monstrous symbiosis of high and low elements, both originating from the hero. One part of him idealises her with out-and-out hyperbolical abstraction; another confusedly seeks to confer real existence on this chimaera amidst a ridiculously prosaic setting and adjuncts. After all, it was he who originally identified her with Aldonza Lorenzo, the good-looking wench of whom he was once secretly enamoured (I, 1) and the prototype of all the travesties. Little reflection is required to see that the inner vision and the outer incarnations belong to each other. Both proceed from a single creative intuition; the extremity of the distance between them is geared to the vision's exaggerated quality, which the incarnations reflect in an inverted mirror of caricature. In this mismatch, as in heaven-made marriages, one side exerts a magnetic pull on the other. No sooner does the hero fantasise about Dulcinea at moonlit balconies than lewd, hunch-backed Maritornes appears at the inn-loft embrasure as though in answer to the summons (I, 43). Madness is the catalyst of this unlikely congress. In the scene just cited, it is responsible both for the fulsome fantasies and for the hero's serene acceptance of Maritornes as a fair rival of his mistress and a suitable object of gallantry. The hero's madness is thus the chief agent of Cervantes's intuition; it continually generates those monstrous 'misappropriations' that Fielding defined as essential to burlesque (see p. 61).

As becomes all too apparent in his conversation with Sancho in I, 25, the Don is quite indifferent to Aldonza as she really is; she is merely a convenient peg in reality on which to hang the ideal. He confesses that his conception of her is all poetic make-believe; the candour is lunatic, not cynical, since it does not prevent him from requesting Sancho in the next breath to deliver a love-letter to this figment. The only potentially persuasive argument that he adduces to justify his choice of her – i.e. that virtue and beauty, rather than rank, are the true movers of love – is surrounded by such crazily frivolous sophistry and glaring contra-dictions as to lack any shred of seriousness (see pp. 67–8). The Sanchopanzine version of Dulcinea, effective basis of the rustic travesties, is the Siamese twin of Quixote's, which he both resists and assimilates. It is just as arbitrary and unreal, despite the fact that Sancho's portrait of Aldonza Lorenzo in I, 25 purports to be based on personal knowledge of her. He offers this version when his master casually lets slip the identity of Dulcinea by naming her parents, mentioning also her illiteracy, her modest upbring-ing, and the 'platonic' (by implication, non-existent) nature of their amatory relationship. Sancho shatters the sentimental effect of this with his portrait: brassy-voiced, weather-tanned, muscu-lar, free with her favours, and faithful to none. Well may his master commit acts of despair for her! What is the point of send-ing conquered foes to her, since they are likely to be mortified to find her threshing flax or winnowing wheat, and she will merely scoff? This character-sketch, which is seminally important, is based on a traditional set-piece of sixteenth-century comedy: the rustic clown's account of his amorous encounter with a strapping wench, whose graces include tossing the caber or bandying obscene insults and whose love-play consists of kicks and scrat-ches. In short, the epitome of unladylike uncouthness.

Just six chapters later (I, 31) Sancho elaborates this portrait when de-briefed by his master after his supposed embassy to Dulcinea. The interrogation takes the form of a high/low anti-phonal; Don Quixote's idealising anticipations or corrections are juxtaposed with Sancho's deflatingly prosaic report of what hap-pened. This too is based on a standard piece of by-play in Golden Age comedy: the master's and servant's systematically contrasted versions of a love-letter or descriptions of a mistress. The dia-logue proceeds thus:

'All that doesn't displease me; carry on', said Don Quixote. 'You arrived, and what was the queen of beauty doing? No doubt you found her stringing pearls or embroidering some device with gold thread for this captive knight of hers.'

'I just found her winnowing some bushels of wheat in a yard of her house', replied Sancho.

'Then imagine that the wheat was grains of pearls, touched by her hands', said Don Quixote. 'And did you look to see if the wheat was *candeal* [the finest quality] or *trechel* [also esteemed]?'

'It was just *rubión* [coarser reddish grain]', replied Sancho.

'Then I assure you that winnowed by her hands it made the very whitest bread, without a doubt', said Don Quixote.   (i, 382)

If Don Quixote, conforming to the master's role in the above mentioned set-piece, idealistically corrects the servant's unworthy account, he also, quite illogically, accepts some of its essentials with serene satisfaction. He does not dispute that she, a princess, was winnowing wheat; he merely quibbles about the quality. True, he will later revise and reject this version of events (II, 8), rhapsodically inviting Sancho to think of Dulcinea as having woven tapestries like the nymphs in Garcilaso's third eclogue. Yet this does not prevent him, immediately afterwards (II, 9), from looking for the palace of princess Dulcinea in the country town of El Toboso, amidst a nocturnal cacophony of barking dogs, grunting pigs, yowling cats. Nor does his idealising tendency prevent him, in mid Part I, from twinning amatory conceits with mention of donkey foals or vulgar anecdotes with comparisons of Dulcinea to Helen and Lucrecia (I, 25). The 'San-chification of Quixote' is no adventitious misfortune; it is congenital to his burlesque make-up.

When the de-briefing is over, Cervantes notes Sancho's relief, 'for though he knew Dulcinea was a peasant girl from El Toboso, he had never seen her in his life' (i, 388). Has Cervantes forgotten what he makes Sancho say in Chapter 25 and imply in Chapter 26? Quite possibly. Yet it is noteworthy that he, or Sancho on his behalf, remembers quite accurately the details of the portrait in I, 25 – e.g. the mortifying discovery of Dulcinea winnowing wheat. So how does he manage to forget the portrait's premise: 'I know her well'? No doubt because the premise is a pretext for Sancho's discharge of a stereotyped function, and Cervantes does not attach much importance to it. There are other implausibilities in Sancho's idea of Dulcinea. Since his description of her in the de-briefing is all a lie, why does he insist provokingly on manly body odour, bread and cheese, coarsest quality wheat? He has already shown himself capable, on occasions, of telling his master what he wants to hear (I, 20). Obviously the functional model predetermines his response. During and after the nocturnal search for Dulcinea in El Toboso (II, 9 and 10), Sancho suffers an even more striking lapse of memory than the one mentioned above. Though he accurately remembers what he said in I, 31, and tries to maintain consistency with it, he forgets altogether about Aldonza Lorenzo's existence (II, 9), and even forgets that Dulcinea is a peasant girl from El Toboso (II, 10). His motive for not discharging his embassy to her is fear of what the angry townsfolk may do to a go-between carrying messages of love to their noble ladies.

Instead, Sancho decides on a subterfuge (II, 10): he will claim that the first country girl sighted at random outside El Toboso is Dulcinea and rely on his master's credulity about enchantment to do the rest. Don Quixote's reaction to this trick shows a marked deviation from his habitual attitude to women in Part I, including some quite as unsavoury as the one chosen by Sancho. Previously, his imagination never failed to convert them into exalted ladies; now, all fired with expectation, it fails. Why? Some obvious reasons of a general nature suggest themselves: he has previously tended to misinterpret *ambivalent* phenomena, and this one is not; moreover, in Part II he tends to see things as they are. Yet there is a more specific set of reasons. The roles of master and squire in this adventure are prefigured by the practical joke in late Part I, modelled on a famous one in Folengo's *Baldus*, in which the pranksters at the inn support Don Quixote's claim that the shaving-basin is the helmet of Mambrino (I, 44–45). The owner of the mundane object is baffled and dismayed to hear them insist in this way. Don Quixote is not the victim on this occasion; yet the practical joke reinforces his convictions about enchantment, giving them a particular twist and predisposing him for the victim's role. The example of the basin-cum-helmet is surely present in his mind when, in early Part II, he retrospectively re-interprets what happened in Sancho's 'embassy' in mid-Part I: 'That was how my lady must have been employed when you saw her [i.e. like the Tagus nymphs], except that some evil enchanter's envious spite against me and mine causes him to change topsy-turvy the shape of things dear to me' (II, 8; ii, 94). The remark puts in Sancho's head the seed of the subterfuge mentioned above. His implementation of it repeats the pattern of the de-briefing in I, 31, where *he* has the active, trickster's part of mediating to his master a rustic version of Dulcinea, while Quixote, with uncharacteristic passivity, sees her in this Sanchopanzine aspect, and tries to gloss or explain away its uncouthness. It also repeats the pattern of the *burla* played on the country-barber. Thus, Quixote's deviation from previous behaviour-patterns in the adventure in II, 10 has a partly natural explanation – the evolution of his notions of enchantment – and a partly artificial one – fugal repetition.

Sancho, implementing his plan, returns to where he left his master outside El Toboso and launches into a virtuoso description of Dulcinea and her damsels – i.e. three rustic wenches who can be seen approaching: 'all glowing with gold, all covered in strings of pearls, all glittering with diamonds and rubies, and wearing brocade more than ten layers deep and hair scattered loose over their shoulders, like so many golden rays playing in the wind' (ii, 108). There is nitwitted excess in this (e.g. the ten-layered brocade), yet it reveals virtually unprecedented panache. Sancho has taken over the role of the clever pranksters: e.g. the priest, mediating between Don Quixote and 'Princess Micomicona' in I, 29. Now follows an altercation which closely repeats, with roles reversed, that preceding Don Quixote's capture of the basin in I, 21 (see p. 64):

'Do you happen to have eyes in the back of your head that you fail to see that I'm talking of these girls approaching, resplendent as the noonday sun?'

'All I see, Sancho . . . are three country girls on three donkeys.'

(11, 109)

This is fugal repetition once more, with an ironic twist which is surely deliberate. The encounter with the girls has a truly theatrical quality thanks to the vivid oppositions of register, posture, and attitude, and the extremities of its irony. Sancho takes the bridle of one wench, and kneeling before her, makes a ceremonious speech of introduction, rendered ridiculous by its botched gradation and epithets: 'Queen, princess, and duchess of beauty, may your haughtiness and greatness deign . . .' The tableau composed of the kneeling and mounted figures is memorably graphic. Don Quixote, with bulging eyes and distraught gaze, confronts the moon-faced, snub-nosed Dulcinea, all graceless and flustered. The language of 'Dulcinea' and her companions is in keeping with her facial expression. It is marked by rustic corruptions and characteristic turns of expression and conveys a coarse, irritated abruptness. In response to Sancho's ridiculously high-flown entreaty to 'Dulcinea' to show pity on the pillar of knight errantry kneeling before her sublime presence, one of Dulcinea's companions exclaims:

'Mas ¡jo, que te estrego, burra de mi suegro! ¡Mirad con qué se vienen los señoritos ahora a hacer burla de las aldeanas, como si aquí no supiésemos echar pullas como ellos! Vayan su camino, y déjenmos pasar, y serles ha sano.' (ii, 110)

'Thanks for the compliment, I'm sure! Look at these toffs trying to make fun of us village girls, as if we couldn't think of some rude names to pay them back with! Be on your way, and let us by, and it will be the better for you.'

'Thanks for the compliment. . .' is a very rough rendering of the Spanish, which literally means 'Whoa, I'm rubbing you down, my father-in-law's donkey!' and signifies 'Don't say thank you!', addressed to an ungrateful person. Here it represents a standard ironic retort by country girls to the compliments or banter of wayfarers. In such encounters, the bandying of witty, obscene insults (*echar pullas*) was common practice. In supposing Sancho to have addressed a *pulla* to 'Dulcinea', the wench has grasped his facetiousness but missed its point: which is parody, not obscenity.

'Déjenmos' and 'nueso' are corruptions of 'déjennos' and 'nuestro'. The contrast between this lumpish rusticity and the ladylike graces anticipated by Don Quixote is extreme; the scene's comic effect hinges on it.

Immediately after this Don Quixote delivers an entreaty to 'Dulcinea' which Auerbach, in a famous essay in *Mimesis* (1953), characterised as lofty, beautiful, grandly periodic. That Auerbach, no sentimentalist about *Don Quixote*, and committed by his very project to 'date' it, should have taken this view shows the difficulty of grasping the nuances of Cervantes's parody now that the period's strong and precise sense of decorum and of rhetorical registers is lost. In II, 18, on the threshold of Don Diego de Miranda's house, the hero is reminded of his enchanted mistress by the sight of some vats from El Toboso and 'without considering what he was saying, nor before whom he was saying it', recites the first two lines of Garcilaso's most famous sonnet – a tender apostrophe to the love-pledges of a dead mistress – and pompously paraphrases and applies them to the vats. The narrator's comment, just cited, is pertinent to his entreaty to Dulcinea, particularly since it begins with two quotations from Garcilaso integrated in the prose: 'Levántate, Sancho . . . que ya veo que *la Fortuna, de mi mal no harta*, tiene tomados los caminos todos por donde pueda venir algún contento a *esta ánima mezquina* que tengo en las carnes' [my emphasis] ('Arise, Sancho, for I now see that Fortune, not surfeited with injuring me, has blocked all the roads by which some contentment can reach this wretched soul that I have within my flesh'). This is as wordily theatrical and self-pitying as the exclamation in II, 18. The elegantly effusive invocation to Dulcinea which follows – 'And thou, O limit of desirable worth, ultimate term of human courtesy, only remedy of this afflicted heart that adores thee!' – is rendered ridiculous by the nature of the addressee and the subsequent insistence on the effects of enchantment on him: the clouds and cataracts in his eyes which cause him to see her as a poor wench. The supplication to her to look gently and amorously upon him, unless he too has been turned into a hateful monster, ends in wordy cacophony: 'echando de ver en esta sumisión y arrodillamiento que a tu contra*hecha he*rmo*su*ra *ha*go, la *hu*milidad con que mi alma te adora' [my emphasis] ('observing in this obeisance and genuflection that I make to thy misshapen beauty the humility with which my soul adores thee'). The italicised dipthongs and assonances would have seemed inept to the ears of Cervantes's contemporaries, sensitive to the weight, measure, and rhymes of rhetorical prose. Cacophony is aggravated by the tendency in old Spanish, not yet extinct in that epoch, to aspirate those 'h's'. The uncouth pomposity of 'esta sumisión y arrodillamiento' is self-evident. The form of this oration is therefore risible; so, obviously, are the circumstances; and the combination of these factors should obviously affect our conception of the emotional content.

In his romantic fiction Cervantes twice presents scenes somewhat analogous to this one: the lover's constancy is tested when his mistress's beauty is horridly disfigured as a result of a witch's spell. In them, the emphasis falls on the spiritual basis of the lover's feelings, unchanged by the mistress's bodily transformation; he shows them by deeds – in one case, a prompt offer of marriage; the calamity's cause is sinister and real and so are the effects. In *Don Quixote* II, 10 the emphasis falls, shatteringly, on 'Dulcinea's' unworthiness; and the calamity is just a ridiculous misapprehension, born of mad credulity. To highlight this is the chapter's purpose, as is made plain by the preamble, in which the narrator expresses his fear that he may not be believed, since Don Quixote's lunacy exceeded by two cross-bow shots the greatest imaginable. My point is that had Cervantes intended to create an effect of pathos, let alone tragedy, as critics like Auerbach suppose, he would have gone about his business in an altogether different way.

The supplication is met, shatteringly, with: '¡Tomá que mi agüelo! . . .¡Amiguita soy yo de oír resquebrajos!' (roughly, 'Strewth, you must be joking! As if I wanted nothing better than to hear you chat me up'), and a curt injunction to get out of the way. So Don Quixote's oratory is left suspended in a vacuum. A similar effect of bathos is achieved by the physical farce of the sequel. 'Dulcinea', released by Sancho, goads her mount so urgently that it bucks and pitches her off. Don Quixote gallantly steps forward to assist her to re-mount, but is forestalled by her unladylike reaction: taking a little run, she vaults, lighter than a falcon, into the saddle where she sits in manly posture, legs astride. That leap will etch itself indelibly on the hero's imagination. After 'Dulcinea' has ridden off, he harps on the unladylike stench of garlic which issued from her mouth, and in the next chapter (II, 11) quibbles with Sancho about his comparison of her eyes to pearls, more appropriate to a fish than a lady. With characteristic irony, Cervantes makes the laments of this persecuted lover fall flat by focusing his attention and ours on deflating trivia.

This gay objectivity has been apparent from the beginning of the adventure. Its dramatic conflicts, so starkly presented, seem to cry out for moral comment, yet the only one that Cervantes offers is an arabesque of wit irrelevant to the burning main issue: who the girls are. He trivialises and partly parodies it with a variant on his practice of mock-punctilious deliberation about the precise name, or form of a name, or species, to be assigned to the object in question, the more footling the better. Here he equivocates about the wenches' donkeys, vacillating between the masculine and feminine (*borrico/borrica; pollino/pollina; jumento/jumenta*), then between the variant feminines. The dialogue between master and squire echoes the equivocation, compounding it with a quibble about the form of *hacaneas* (palfreys), which Sancho, referring to the three mounts, mispronounces as *cananeas*. Since for the seventeenth-century lexicographer Covarrubias *borrico, pollino,* and *jumento* are interchangeable synonyms, the prevarication is risibly pointless. Yet it carries a mutely eloquent comment on the absurd unseriousness of this imbroglio. For Auerbach, Cervantes's playfulness is tantamount to an aesthetic bracketing-out of substantial moral problems. In my view, the comedy of Don Quixote's attitude to Dulcinea has an implicit moral; the story of the Cave of Montesinos helps to clarify it.

No episode in *Don Quixote* has elicited such a diversity of speculative interpretation as this one; the standpoints include the metaphysical, Freudian, existential, mystic, autobiographical, and more besides. A representative example of this variety is Percas de Ponsetti's long, subtle and erudite reading (1975 [II, 407–583]), which takes the story as nothing less than a universal allegory of the human psyche, implicit in an acute study of Don Quixote's attempts to externalise, part subconsciously, the mixed motives of doubt, lucidity, and self-delusion induced by the trauma of Dulcinea's enchantment. Without wishing to deny the story's complexity and allusiveness, I propose to take as guidelines of interpretation the narrator's evaluation, the hero's motivation as manifest in the text (rather than the texts of modern psychoanalysis), the novel's leitmotifs, and parallels in other Cervantine works.

The motives for the story, and the state of mind revealed by it, seem in one respect enigmatic, and in others, exceptional; yet I shall argue that they are fundamentally consistent with the Don's make-up as revealed hitherto. The consistency helps to clarify the enigma, or at least, to dimish it. By means of his story (II, 23), Don Quixote receives answers to two questions that have been nagging him since the encounter with the wenches outside El Toboso: whether it is Dulcinea herself, or merely his perception of her, that is afflicted, and how she is to be disenchanted. He also fully reconciles that encounter to his chivalric world, thus fulfilling one of his primordial motives: to reassure himself that the indignities that befall him are the common lot of famous knights-errant. In the cave he hobnobs with one of the heroes of the Carolingian ballads, Montesinos, who treats him with fulsome courtesy. His visit culminates in the sight of Dulcinea as she appeared in the recent meeting with her. Though most of his narrative is taken up with the misfortunes of Montesinos, Durandarte, and Belerma, its structure presupposes that these prefigure Dulcinea's, just as in Garcilaso's third eclogue (cited by him in connection with Dulcinea in II, 8) the tapestries of mythological tragedies of love build up to the tapestry of Elisa's death and incorporate it in the legendary pantheon. On seeing Dulcinea, he learns from his guide Montesinos that this must be one of many principal ladies who have been brought to this underworld reserve by Merlin in strange and diverse shapes. So Dulcinea is in good company; if she is enchanted, so are all the heroes and heroines of this Valhalla. Most gratifyingly, he hears that he is the knight destined to break the spell.

The story is at the hub of Don Quixote's relation to Dulcinea, which involves Sancho too. Once the Duchess gets to hear of the adventure of the Cave from Sancho (II, 33), the way is open for the adventure of the enchanted carts (II, 35), in which 'Merlin', impersonated by the Duke's majordomo, appears to Don Quixote and Sancho and imposes the conditions for Dulcinea's release: 3,300 lashes to be applied by Sancho to his own buttocks. Sancho, just previously (II, 33), has been gulled into believing that the wench outside El Toboso really was the enchanted Dulcinea. So the wheel comes full circle for both heroes. Sancho is caught in the web of the lies that he began to weave in mid Part I. Don Quixote's attempts to be admitted to Dulcinea's presence, which effectively began in mid Part I amidst burlesque self-mortification, bare buttocks and shirt tails, theatrical laments and doggerel verse, blackmail, lies, and prosaic inducements, end in the same inglorious way. In its very basis, Don Quixote's relation to Dulcinea is a crazily exuberant story or poem (see p. 90), which he improvises under the pressure of events and other people's awkward questions. Thus, the story of the Cave, if it is no more than that, conforms essentially to that basis, differing only in its deliberate inventiveness. Madness completely blurs the difference. How does one tell 'deliberate' from 'undeliberate' in a madman?

The narrative is a major example of fugal repetition: the Sanchopanzine Dulcinea created in mid Part I is now thoroughly absorbed in Don Quixote's vision: not as his conception of what his mistress is intrinsically, but of her enchanted plight. The image of an apparently uncouth, hopping, malodorous Dulcinea obsesses him henceforth. Moreover, he turns the chivalric Elysium of the cave into a fit place for the Sanchopanzine Dulcinea to inhabit. There is no inconsistency in this, no lapse from a supposedly normal, elevated conception of chivalry. Nor is there inconsistency between his wonder-struck delight in the vision and the unworthiness of the Cave's inmates. He feels compassion for them, to be sure; but this is caused by their misfortunes as enchanted beings, not by their lapses of taste, which he fails to notice and freely shares.

In order to argue that there is inconsistency, one might make a contrast between the story of the Knight of the Lake (I, 50; see pp. 68–9) and that of the Cave; the first is obviously a precursor of the second, and, as we have seen, has a quality of precious luxuriance. It features Elysian fields, an enchanted castle, a procession of damsels – all repeated in the sequel. In this, the chivalric personages have the requisite status and partly suitable emotions (awe, grief, solemnity), but degrade them by their aspects, language, indecorous banality. If we consider the manner of degradation, we find that it often sustains leitmotifs initiated by Don Quixote himself or consonant with his mentality. His anachronistic portrait of Montesinos, guardian of the Alice-in-Wonderland inferno, and originally a hero of the ballad-tradition, shows him dressed in black round bonnet, green scholars' sash, and purple gown (the *bayeta*, often used for mourning), with a rosary of outsize beads. The effect of this get-up is antique, sanctimonious, and clerical. It is quite consonant with Don Quixote's habit of giving disconcertingly familiar, idiosyncratic sketches of his literary idols: c.g. bandy-legged, blond-bearded, swarthy Roland (II, 1). His and Montesinos's amusing indelicacy about the physical functions of enchanted persons repeats the substance and tone of the conversation that he had with Sancho in I, 48–49. In describing Dulcinea and her companions, he gives a bizarrely Quixotic inflexion to their Sanchopanzine characteristics, in accord with his own literary bent and peculiar notions of enchantment's topsy-turvy effects. In relating that he saw three peasant girls leaping and skipping like goats ('*saltando* y brincando como *cabras*' [ii, 220; my emphasis]) over those Elysian

fields, he performs a surrealistic pun on Sancho's original description of Dulcinea's vault over her mount's rear crupper ('el arzón
trasero de la silla pasó de un *salto*') and of her departure as swift
as a zebra ('hace correr la hacanea como una *cebra*' [II, 10; ii,
111; my emphasis]). With the mention of goats and Elysian fields,
he transposes Dulcinea's famous leap into a mythological, Virgilian key. Her arrow-like escape from him not only reminds us of
the wench's behaviour in II, 10, but of Dido's abrupt, resentful
flight from Aeneas when he tries to speak to her in the underworld (*Aeneid* VI). Thus the notion that the vision in the cave is
out of character must be rejected. Its degradation is unusual in
degree, but not in kind. The reason for the increase in degree is
that, down there in the cave, Quixote's madness is not joined to
its Siamese twin (e.g. Aldonza, Maritornes), but must create it
spontaneously.

To elicit the story's latent 'moral' – obviously it has no overt
one – we must take account of its fantastic inventiveness and
surrealistic imagery, which shed light on the link between Don
Quixote's attitude to Dulcinea and two kinds of manic obsession
or enthusiasm which are depicted over and over again in Cervantes's works. They make up a family of aberrations, both moral
and artistic in nature; Cervantes's concern with them is personally
motivated. It takes one to know one.

The story of the cave is told to an audience consisting of Sancho
and the guide, a facetious scholar who is preparing a burlesque
version of Ovid's *Metamorphoses* about the legendary geneses of
some notable, and notably mundane, Spanish landmarks. What
impresses this pair is not the story's degraded quality but its
impossibility; this scepticism reflects the author's preoccupations
about its deviation from the novel's basic principle. Yet with what
nonchalant levity he expresses them! He devolves them onto his
characters, causing them inconclusively to bat the pros and cons
back and forth. This whimsical incorporation in the novel of its
mechanics of composition is characteristic of Cervantes. His non-
chalance eloquently implies his priorities: with so superbly out-

landish a story, who cares about the precise motives or cause?
After all, with a madman anything goes.

The characters involved in the debate are, apart from those
mentioned, Don Quixote and Benengeli; the latter's doubts are
aired in the preamble to Chaper 24. Their opinion, including Don
Quixote's up to a point, reveal unanimity; though idiosyncrat-
ically and humorously expressed, they deserve to be given
weight. For Benengeli, as for Sancho and the guide, there are
just two possibilities: either Don Quixote saw what he claims to
have seen or he is lying. None of these characters entertains the
notion that modern critics tend to assert with dogmatic conviction: that the vision was a dream or hallucination. The grounds
for this view are, amongst others, that the hero emerges from the
cave in a state of impervious slumber, and later in Part II, when
harking back to the story, suggests that it may have been a dream.
Eventually Cervantes flippantly severs the Gordian knot by making Benengeli incline to the second alternative – a lie – on the
basis of definite reports of a death-bed recantation by Don
Quixote. However, this solution is to some extent deprived of
finality by the Moor's previous tongue-in-cheek assertions about
the hero's unimpeachable integrity and the difficulty of his having
invented so great a pack of nonsense in so short a time.
Benengeli's puzzlement is transmitted to the hero, who in II,
25 and 62 consults oracles in order to determine whether the
experience in the cave was real or dreamed. The fact that both
oracles are fraudulent does nothing to inspire a sense of the problem's seriousness. Even more devastating are the implications
of the hero's Parthian shot to Sancho at the end of II, 41: 'Sancho,
since you want to be believed about what you saw in the sky, I
want you to believe me about what I saw in the cave of Montesinos. I say no more' (ii, 355). By offering to exchange his acquiescence in Sancho's transparent lies about what he saw from
Clavileño's back for Sancho's acquiescence in the story of the
cave, he implicitly puts both stories on the same footing. This
would imply that the whole edifice of his love for Dulcinea is a

fake; more directly, it supports Benengeli's suggestion that the story of the Cave was an invention.

A pack of nonsense, maybe, but superbly inventive nonetheless. In it, the hero reveals the same delight in spinning chivalric yarns and the same exuberant wit as on previous occasions. This is the old trouper's greatest act, and his enjoyment is visceral: he enjoys a hearty *merienda* before launching into it. He thus conforms to a character-type who holds a particular fascination for Cervantes: the tall-story teller, partly emblematic of the fictional narrator. This figure relates dreams, or fantasies with a dream-like aspect, as though they were things really witnessed. In *Persiles* II, 15, the hero, Periandro, recounts his dream of what he saw on a paradisal island: two allegorical processions, of which the first represents Sensuality and the second Chastity, personified by his beloved Auristela. As this example suggests, dreams, for Cervantes, tend to be allegorical revelations of the dreamer's over-riding preoccupations and give an insight into their moral essence. Considered as delightful stories they have a further aspect. About Periandro's dream one of his listeners says: 'Those are powers of the imagination, in which things apprehended from memory are represented with such vehemence that, though false, they appear true.'

In the story of the cave, this vehemence is characterised by a surrealistic quality: that is, minute particularity about bizarre phenomena and an effect of sensorial immediacy. These features, together with its Lewis Carroll-like caprice and its dense literary allusiveness, give the story's fantasy its distinctive tone. The narrative technique partly resembles that of E.A. Poe's tales of the supernatural, in which technical precision about distances and sensations lends an air of realism to incredible prodigies. Don Quixote begins thus: 'At about the depth of twelve or fourteen times the height of an average man, on the right hand side, there is a concavity and space capable of containing a large cart with its team of mules. It is lit by a pale light descending from cracks or holes in the earth's surface which communicate with it from afar. . .' (ii, 211). Soon there follows the memorable passage in which Don Quixote, having woken from a deep sleep to find himself in a field of paradisal beauty, reports his struggle with his own incredulity and his tests to make sure that he was not dreaming: 'I blinked my eyes and rubbed them; I saw that I wasn't dreaming, but was really awake; nonetheless, I felt my head and chest, to find out if it was I who was there or some vain and counterfeit fantasm; but my sense of touch, my feelings, and my coherent reasoning convinced me that I was the very same there and then as I am now.' The implications of this passage have to do with the novelist's power to visualise and his struggle with his critical conscience. Another Cervantine tall-story teller, the narrator of the short story *The Dogs' Colloquy*, likewise speaks of the struggle between his rational scepticism and the clear recollection of having been in full possession of his faculties. Like Don Quixote, he insists on the truth of what he saw. And like him, he is confronted by a sceptical audience, the voice of rational incredulity; the division doubtless corresponds to one that Cervantes felt within himself. With regard to Don Quixote's narrative, the ironic role is discharged by Sancho and the guide, who, by their quibbling doubts and questions, convey not just scepticism but debunking facetiousness. Their concern with inconsequential minutiae – e.g. 'That dagger must have been manufactured by Ramón de Hoces of Seville'; 'Do enchanted people eat?' – is matched, in an innocently solemn key, by Don Quixote and Montesinos within the narrative itself – e.g. 'his heart must have weighed two pounds, because, according to natural philosophy, the greater one's heart the greater one's courage' (ii, 214).

Don Quixote chiefly reveals his virtuosity by his complex interweaving of strands of literary allusion, in which the Ovidian strand predominates. For the Renaissance, Ovid was the masterspinner of fables; Quixote *fabulator* is thus aiming for supremacy in the highest league. His story is a sequel to a couple of traditional ballads about Durandarte's request to Montesinos, as he lies dying on the field of Roncesvalles, to cut out his heart and take it to his mistress. They are notable for their pathetic and

declamatory style, their gruesomeness, and their curious punctiliousness about the small dagger used for the autopsy and the
grave-digging. These features invite parody; and others besides
Cervantes rose to the challenge: notably Góngora, in an aggress-
ively demeaning sequel picturing Belerma's mourning. Other
strands in the tapestry are provided by folklore and the geography
of La Mancha: legends linking Montesinos to a ruined castle near
the cave and the geographical facts of the vicinity of the cave to
the lagoons of Ruidera, feeding the partly subterranean river
Guadiana. Out of all this, Don Quixote creates a burlesque of
Ovid's *Metamorphoses*, thus emulating in advance, without
deliberate flippancy, the spoof projected by his guide. In Don
Quixote's version of the *Ovidio español*, Merlin is the agent of
prodigious metamorphosis. Thanks to him, the personages of the
ballads haunt the cave in enchanted form. Montesinos's grief-
stricken account of these prodigies has a pedestrian homeliness,
which anticipates the tone of Teresa Panza's letter to her husband
(II, 52), full of the latest village news. There are delightful
touches here: e.g. the mention of Durandarte's mournful squire
'Guadiana' and Belerma's *dueña* 'Ruidera', together with her
seven daughters and two nieces. None of these personages are
featured in the ballads. They are conjured up by Cervantes, or
derived from popular lore, in order to 'explain' the genesis of the
subterranean river and the lagoons. When Montesinos reveals to
Durandarte the prospect of deliverance by Don Quixote, Durandarte replies bathetically with a catchphrase expressive of shoul-
der-shrugging resignation (ii, 217): 'Y cuando así no sea . . .
paciencia y barajar' ('and should that not be so, patience and
shuffle the cards'). This lamely questioning or domestic note,
juxtaposed with supernatural prodigy, is insistent in the story.

By means of it, and his chivalric delusion in general, Don Quixote reveals his kinship to the most commonly encountered of
Cervantes's character-types: the head-in-clouds fantasist,
obsessed by his *idée fixe*. I refer particularly to two works which
portray this figure: the poem, *Voyage to Parnassus*, and the comedy, *Jealousy's Abode*. The poem is a whimsical allegory about

the good poets' defence of Parnassus against the poetasters; Cervantes finds himself involved when he journeys to Parnassus in quest of the poetic inspiration that he has always lacked. His self-portrait as an impulsive, ambitious, ever-hopeful poet, undaunted by white hairs and repeated disillusionment, is drawn near the beginning and becomes thematic. In Chapter 6 he relates his vision of Vainglory: a monstrous giantess, fair only when seen from afar, pot-bellied with wind, and attended by the maidens Adulation and Lies. This dream is preceded by an explanation of the causes of dreams, to be sought in the dreamer's (i.e. Cervantes's own) over-riding preoccupation. The vision is emblematic of the whole story of the voyage, which gives ironically self-conscious expression to its creator's thirst for status and recognition, symbolising it in a fantastic trip to mythological wonderland. Thus, barring the self-consciousness, it has some affinity with the story of the cave, and resembles it further in the gently debunking quality of its humour: surrealistic, capricious, grotesque, and mundane.

Jealousy's Abode is a sort of allegorical spectacular, based on Boiardo's and Ariosto's heroic poems, about Roland's and Rinaldo's frenzied pursuit of Angelica through the forest of the Ardennes and the efforts of the enchanter Malgesí to stop them, or bring them to their senses, by means of hallucinatory shocks and magical impediments. One of these prodigies is Rinaldo's vision of the abode of jealousy, a cavernous serpent's maw rather similar to the cave of Montesinos; Malgesí, personifying Horror, is the guardian, and he introduces Rinaldo to the abode's other inmates, likewise emblematic of Rinaldo's disordered soul. Jealousy, last to be introduced, shakes hands with Rinaldo, whose breast is simultaneously scorched and frozen. Yet no salutary effect ensues. Malgesí's magic works merely as a fleeting, awesome hallucination, it makes no impact on free human will. Like the stereotyped bad magician of pantomime, he is left baffled by his failure. His other prodigies have a typically degraded and bathetic quality and a similarly emblematic function. They have a specific and general pertinence to *Don Quixote*. Specifically, they suggest that the prodigies of the cave of Montesinos are symptomatic of the tortuous, diseased, self-perpetuating nature of the hero's madness, with all its chimerical claptrap about enchantment. Generally, they shed light on the failure of the remedies tried on Don Quixote: not magic, but persuasion, trickery, and force. Cervantes's fascination with his hero is due to the general representativeness of his madness, which, besides its literary implications, stands for all the passions and obsessions that Cervantes feared and despised in himself and in others: the desire for fame, presumption, impulsiveness, belligerence, literary excess. The humour of *Don Quixote* is symptomatic of a rationalist's attempt to domesticate the monsters of unreason by laughter. Their power, and potential sinisterness, come from the human mind's endless capacity for self-delusion. Hence they can only be defeated after a long painful process of *self*-enlightenment. Instant remedies, applied from without, don't work. In this sense, the story of the cave may be seen as a necessary step towards enlightenment. Don Quixote's futile obsession with Dulcinea and chivalry must work itself out until all its tortuous possibilities are exhausted; only then, confronted by the final blank wall of his self-made labyrinth, can he exclaim: '*Malum sigum*! *Malum signum*! Liebre huye; galgos la siguen; ¡Dulcinea no parece!' ('Bad omen! Bad omen! Hare flies; greyhounds pursue it; Dulcinea won't appear' [*DQ* II, 73; ii, 581; see p. 84]).

Chapter 3

'Don Quixote' as landmark

Don Quixote, as Cervantes and his contemporaries saw it, was a long work of comedy designed to ridicule chivalric romances. No ambiguity envelops that judgement; nor, apparently, was there uncertainty about the theoretical basis of Cervantes's critique; nor, one surmises, would there have been much confusion about the moral and socially satiric themes of his novel, since these accord with the ideology of the age. Yet, since the late eighteenth century, posterity has insistently cast doubt on Cervantes's intentions, discovered deep ambiguities or inconsistencies in his novel's conceptual core, and invested it with meanings that he would have found difficult to comprehend, let alone endorse. That transformation has affected not only the novel's 'message' but also the artistic form in which that message is distilled. Posterity has re-created *Don Quixote*, fashioning it in the image of its changing life-philosophies, aesthetic values, and artistic styles and themes. I began this book by saying that *Quixote* criticism has been intimately involved in this process; I end it by showing how the process has been reflected in the genre of the novel. To a certain extent, the critics have simply followed the novelists' lead.

The basic motive behind this kind of re-creation of old books is inseparable from our curiosity about them, and, to my mind, inherently natural and proper: the urge to discover their potential relevance to our own experience. There are limits beyond which the quest for relevance becomes excessive – limits for the literary critic rather than the creative artist – and I shall refer to them in the concluding paragraph. In the foregoing pages, I have frequently drawn attention to features in *Don Quixote* which seem to encourage the quest: its air of being a satiric fable with sugges-

109

tive overtones, like Rabelais's *Gargantua* and *Pantagruel*; the quasi-epic nature of the hero's rebellion against social order and common sense; his elusive switching between crazy but stylish heroics, infantile aberration, specious semi-lucidity, genuine wisdom; Cervantes's non-committal irony; above all, perhaps, his deliberate generality or universality of reference. Three themes or aspects of *Don Quixote* in particular were destined to appear to posterity as an exemplary pre-figuration of its concerns: first, the conflict between the subjective imagination and the real world; secondly, the question of art's mimetic relation to life, and thirdly, that of its relation to preceding traditions and enabling conventions.

Erich Heller, in *The Disinherited Mind* (1952), has written of the Western European mind's loss, since the Renaissance, of a 'sacramental' sense of the unity of the spiritual and natural spheres. Emancipated from its theocentric world-view, Western thought has become increasingly confident about answering questions as to *how* nature works, and at the same time, increasingly diffident about saying *what* it signifies. The search for ultimate answers has devolved on poets, visionaries, and religious believers, and has been accompanied, at least amongst the poets, by familiar Romantic feelings of stigmatised alienation. The mind thus 'disinherited' has restlessly tried to cope with the schism between knowledge and transcendental longings, or physical necessity and spiritual creativity. Such, in brief outline, is the background to posterity's concern with the opposition of the Ideal and the Real in *Don Quixote*. As I have already suggested (pp. 42–3), this kind of approach is out of alignment with Cervantes's world-view, which presupposes that the Great Chain of Being linking God to creatures is still in place, the symbolic Book of Nature revealing God in creatures is still decipherable. If man feels alienated from transcendent truth, or finds disaccord between aspiration and fulfilment, or sees the world as a labyrinth of confusion, this is basically due to his own moral confusion. This is the latent implication of the opposition between subjective imagination and reality in *Don Quixote*; its specific aim, of course, is to mock imagination's literary delusions by confronting them with hard facts, which are presumed, in a robustly common-sensical way, to be intelligible.

The 'problem of mimesis', the second of the three exemplary themes mentioned above, is obviously related in a general way to the first theme. Yet it is also explained by other factors: notably, the European novel's development of increasingly soph-isticated methods of mimetic representation from the eighteenth century onwards, which led, at the beginning of the twentieth century, to a sense of surfeit and scepticism about the whole project. This process of sophistication also explains the novel's attitude of ironic and self-conscious introversion – theme number three – which became established as part of the narrator's persona from the genre's origins onwards. To what extent may Cervantes be regarded as an authentic precursor of these preoccupations? The answer is: to a more limited extent than is typically asserted. Thus, in *Don Quixote*, he is basically concerned with the need for heroic romance to respect the basic rules of classical art, particularly verisimilitude; he is not bothered by more radical aspects of the 'problem of mimesis': e.g. the self-evidently thorny implications of the concept 'imitation of nature'.

I make such qualifications in order to prompt a fitting sense of *admiratio*, too easily prompted by invocations of prophetic genius. It ought to appear astonishing that Cervantes, whose intellectual environment was very far removed from that of most of his subsequent imitators in the genre of prose-fiction, should nonetheless have appeared to them as being so inspiringly access-ible. The reasons for this accessibility lie elsewhere than in the overlap, real or imagined, between his thematic preoccupations and theirs. To give posterity its due, it has clearly acknowledged these reasons. First, Cervantes was a supreme master of narra-tive, in all the forms and styles known to his age; on this technical level – e.g. handling of reunions and recognitions, use of sus-pense, variation of pace and moods, interpolations – *Don Quix-ote* left a palpable imprint on the European novel until well into the nineteenth century. Dickens is one of his most obvious debtors in this respect. Secondly, his handling of comedy in all its manifold aspects – parody, characterisation, ironic situations, farce, the narrator's humorous persona – was a quarry that his successors mined freely; the range of indebtedness goes from Fielding's rumbustious bedroom scenes to the delicate ironies implicit in the prattle of Mark Twain's Huck Finn and Jim. Thirdly, Cervantes's mastery of the registers of language and style, perceptible even in translation, provided a lesson in virtuosity and, not least, the mixing and expansion of generic themes and modes; the fruits are plainly visible in Sterne and Melville, and, arguably, in James Joyce. Fourthly, his portrayal of Don Quixote and Sancho, with all that it implied for the subsequent treatment of character in the genre of the novel (see p. 53), was obviously the most important lesson of all. Cervantes touched an archetypal spring here, which, as is the way with great myths, would inspire and still continues to inspire a prodigious quantity and range of creative activity: Kozintsev's film with Cherkassov in the title-role; songs by Ravel; a ballet by Roberto Gerhard; operas by Mendelssohn, Donizetti, Massenet; illustrations by Dali and Picasso; Richard Strauss's tone-poem; Graham Greene's *Monsignor Quixote*; Robin Chapman's *The Duchess's Diary*; Dale Wasserman's musical *Man of La Mancha*; laser-generated cartoon-games of Don Quixote's adventures; helmet of Mambrino ash-trays. I am informed that in the peaceful insurrection of the population of the Philippines against the Marcos dictatorship in 1986, the rebels' 'battle-hymn' was Wasserman's 'The Impossible Dream' – Don Quixote's theme-song. Has any other literary figment shown such power to mobilise the masses?

I turn now to the story of posterity's reception and re-creation of *Don Quixote*, with the preliminary qualification that to pursue its ghost through Western literature, particularly the novel, after 1615, virtually involves re-writing that literature's history. Though very popular in the seventeenth century, *Don Quixote* was regarded as a broad, coarse-grained work of comedy, as is evident from its imitations: e.g. Avellaneda's sequel to Part I (1614) and Butler's *Hudibras* (1663). Hence it was not yet placed on the pedestal of classical status. It earned this distinction in the first half of the eighteenth century; the process began in England, with France not lagging far behind. Spain followed suit in the century's last quarter. There were scholarly editions and biographies; rival translations; paintings and illustrations; admiring mentions of Cervantes – by Addison, Warburton, Pope, Dr Johnson, Voltaire – in any context dealing with satire, humour, and burlesque; wide approval of his civilised decorum; Quixotic allusions in French revolutionary pamphlets; plays, novels, ballets, operas, pantomines, firework-displays with Quixotic themes. In 1780, the Royal Spanish Academy brought out an edition of *Don Quixote* with an introduction by Vicente de los Ríos, which claims for Cervantes a status in the genre of satiric burlesque equivalent to Homer's and Virgil's in epic poetry. The neo-classical view expressed in this introduction, with its appeal to wholesome reason and good taste, the imitation of nature, universally valid rules, was broadly typical of the century.

So, appreciation of *Don Quixote* had become more refined by comparison with that of the seventeenth century, yet had not fundamentally changed. However, from the mid-century onwards, a significant counter-trend began to resist the prevalent tide of opinion; and Henry Fielding was one of its initiators. In *Joseph Andrews* (1742), Fielding explicity avows the intention of imitating the manner of Cervantes: i.e. his mock-grave burlesque style, much admired in that period, and, no doubt, his jocular drawing of attention to the conventions of story-telling, which Fielding carries much further. For reasons already mentioned, he disavows any intention of copying the character of Don Quixote (see p. 61) yet it is obvious that he had derived inspiration from this source in depicting Parson Adams: learned, good-natured, judicious, generous, brave to a fault, and – in extravagant degree – innocent and unworldly. Parson Adams conforms to the type of 'the amiable humorist' (Stave 1960), who would proliferate from the mid-century onwards, and provokes a response very different from the contemptuous laughter described by Hobbes. His 'humour' or hobby-horse makes him simultaneously absurd and lovable. The best known example is Sterne's Uncle Toby. Gently compassionate towards all creation – even flies and the devil – diffident wooer of Widow Wadman, indefatigable debater of abstruse questions, Toby is governed by a passion which assorts very oddly with his peaceable nature: he re-lives his military past by playing with model fortifications on a specially adapted bowling-green. His affinities with Don Quixote are obvious.

Of the major eighteenth-century novels, Sterne's *Tristram Shandy* (1759) is the one most infused with a Cervantine spirit. A superb shaggy dog story, it is a novel about writing a novel; throughout it, the present tense of writing, lived by the narrator, tends to get confused with the 'life and opinions' that are supposedly the subject of narration. I say 'supposedly' because most of the narrative is occupied by Tristram's pre-history and early upbringing, and the lives and opinions of other members of the Shandy family and circle: notably, his father Walter Shandy, Uncle Toby, Toby's servant Corporal Trim. Sterne's irony is reminiscent of Cervantes in all sorts of ways: the persistent contrast between his narrator's public, social address to a genteel readership and the trifling oddity of the subject-matter; the gentle debunking of all kinds of learned pretensions, exemplified by Walter Shandy's metaphysical theories about the properties of names and noses; the insistent juxtaposition of the imaginative or rational and the physical. A memorable example of this juxtaposition is the novel's opening, in which Walter Shandy's monthly performance of his conjugal duty is interrupted by his wife's question whether he has remembered to wind the clock. We should note in passing that Sterne's joyous liberties with sexual decorum are *not*, alas, typical of Cervantes. The passage just mentioned, and the novel's playful reflexivity in general, illustrate Sterne's radical extension of the potentialities of Cervantine irony. Whereas Cervantes invites us to measure irrationality – whether lived or literary – against a prudent norm, Sterne gently implies that we are all engaged in projecting Shandy-like constructs on the world, and that in relation to our hobby-horses, any aspect of life, particularly the sexual urge, may be Sancho Panza. Moreover, Tristram's urgent, continually deflected striving to get his life's story across is symbolic of human inarticulateness in general; cross-purposes, the conventions of signs and language, and verbal ambiguities continually skew the attempt to communicate. In *Tristram Shandy*, that lesson is applied with particular emphasis to literary styles and conventions; no novel written before the twentieth century subjects them to such radical questioning.

The neo-classical view of *Don Quixote* was subverted around 1800 by the German Romantic movement, which took the book as a model for the genre that it would proclaim as its own: the novel. For the Romantics – Friedrich and August Wilhelm Schlegel, Schelling, Tieck, Jean Paul Richter – *Don Quixote* was a supreme artistic achievement, on a par with Shakespeare's plays. They admired it for its poetry, its bitter-sweet attitude to Medieval Chivalry, its mythic universality; they identified its theme with their own interpretation of man's predicament and the historical process: the opposition between mind and nature, spirit and nature, tending endlessly towards synthesis. It exemplified Romantic Irony in all its forms: the artist's sense of the gap between Ideal and Real, his mockery of cherished illusions, his playful detachment from his own creation. The cult of Cervantes is not merely exemplified by the Romantic generation's essays, lectures, philosophical and aesthetic writings, but also by the novels of Richter, the short stories of Kleist, E.T.A. Hoffman, and Tieck, and Heine's poetry. The generation's revaluation of *Don Quixote* quickly communicated itself to writers outside Germany – Wordsworth, Coleridge, Byron, de Vigny, Victor Hugo – and was turned into the academic commonplaces of literary history. It was to have a major impact on the nineteenth-century novel in its most prolific period: about 1840 to 1890.

Though the Romantics had signposted the way, the novelists who came after them approached *Don Quixote* in a spirit of personal discovery. Flaubert said of it that it was a book in which he recognised his origins and which he knew by heart even before he could read. Dostoevsky and Victor Hugo paid their homage in even more fulsome terms. A short list of major novels indebted to Cervantes might consist of Dickens's *The Pickwick Papers* (1836–37), Stendhal's *The Charterhouse of Parma* (1839), Herman Melville's *Moby Dick* (1853), Flaubert's *Madame Bovary* (1856–57), Dostoevsky's *The Idiot* (1868), George Eliot's *Middlemarch* (1871), Leopoldo Alas's *The Regentess* (1884), Mark Twain's *The Adventures of Huckleberry Finn* (1885), Galdós's *Doña Perfecta* (1876) and *Fortunata and Jacinta* (1886–87). The influence of *Don Quixote* on Galdós – Spain's greatest novelist after Cervantes – persists throughout his prolific career. One can infer this from *Doña Perfecta*, where *all* the inhabitants of the provincial town of Orbajosa compensate for the empty tedium of their lives by elaborating Quixotic fantasies about themselves: thus, though they habitually indulge in malicious gossip and all kinds of dishonourable misdemeanour, this does not prevent them from seeing themselves as epitomes of well-bred honour. In *Fortunata and Jacinta*, Maxi's relation to the heroine, Fortunata, is modelled on Don Quixote's to Dulcinea, and reveals Galdós's fascination with mental abnormality. A deformed, sickly, and shy chemistry-student, Maxi conceives a spiritually exalted love for Fortunata, living at the time as a street-prostitute. Quixotically transformed by his passion, he marries her and plans to redeem her; his failure drives him mad. Yet even in madness he shows manic logic and lucid, if metaphysically abstract idealism. Cervantes supplied Galdós with a basic model for his delineation of the Spanish character.

Cervantes's formula, as the nineteenth-century novelists perceived it, has been variously defined by Levin (1957), Trilling (1961), and Girard (1965). It may roughly be summarised thus: an epic story of a character fired with illusions which are pitted against the disillusioning facts of social life and end in moral awakening. The epic scale appealed to the nineteenth century's thirst for grand metaphysical, historical, sociological, or moral designs; the opposition of illusion and reality proved a subtle instrument for analysing the complexities of moral experience;

the location of passion and heroism on the stage of Vanity Fair
satisfied both the need to tell a story and the century's historicist
and sceptical mentality. Filled with sociological pretensions, the
novelists aimed to analyse the social fabric in its broad sweep and
minute detail. The resulting variations on the Quixotic theme
produced a momentous expansion of its potentialities. I shall
illustrate these points with reference to Flaubert and Melville.

Flaubert said of great literary characters, such as Don Quixote,
that they illuminate some general truth about human nature;
Emma Bovary is a striking illustration of this notion; she has
given a name to a psychological condition: *bovarysme*. Emma is
a woman whose febrile appetite for emotional fulfilment is viti-
ated by her stereotyped, absolute, self-indulgent preconceptions
of what it involves. These are based on romantically escapist
literature, and more generally, clichés. If Emma's motives thus
appear similar to Don Quixote's delusion, they differ in their
normality. Her habit of thinking and speaking in commonplaces
is repeated on various levels: it is sentimentally duplicated by her
second lover Léon and contrasted by the 'enlightened' attitudes
of the apothecary Homais, which are, in their different way,
equally banal. Flaubert shows, by implication, an exacting and
self-conscious attitude towards the relation of art to its subject-
matter; while aiming to represent his subject with the maximum
of artistic honesty, he also aims to achieve by style and form the
beauty that it naturally lacks. In various ways the settings and
secondary characters of *Madame Bovary* echo and transform the
motifs of *Don Quixote*, endowing them with a sociological representativeness, which, insofar as it is present in Cervantes's novel,
is largely an accidental effect. The small country-town of Yon-
ville, evocative of that anonymous place in La Mancha, is a micro-
cosm of French provincial society: doctor, store-keeper,
apothecary, priest, tax-collector. The social panorama extends
from the riches of an aristocratic ball to drab small-holdings
round Rouen (*cf.* the Duke's palace and the rural scenarios in
Don Quixote). In the pairing of the parish-priest Bournisien and
Homais (*cf.* Cervantes's priest and barber), Flaubert opposes

two dominant contemporary currents of opinion, traditional Catholicism and lay anti-clericalism. Flaubert's irony, in some ways manifestly influenced by Cervantes's, is yet another instance of this kind of transformation. When he splices Rodolphe's wooing of Emma with the orotund speechifying at the agricultural fair, the effect is highly comic; one thinks of Quixote's stilted speech to the goat-herds on the virtues of the Golden Age, or Cervantes's contrasts between coarse rusticity and pastoral affectation. When, during the description of Emma's death-throes, Flaubert juxtaposes them with the blind-man's ditty of young love, evocative of Emma's adulteries, the effect is brutal. The theme of man's lack of self-lucidity and of mastery over his own desires has its equivalent in *Don Quixote*; yet Flaubert's bitterly implacable, and also poignant, inflection of it is quite un-Cervantine.

The notable influence of *Don Quixote* on the American novel is perhaps explained by the fact that certain well-known American myths are easily adaptable to a Quixotic mould. Manifest in the works of Nathaniel Hawthorne, Herman Melville, and Mark Twain, it persists residually in the fiction of Henry James (e.g. *The Ambassadors* [1903]) and in several best-sellers of more recent times: James Farrell's Studs Lonigan trilogy, (1932–35) Hemingway's *A Farewell to Arms* (1929), Scott Fitzgerald's *The Great Gatsby* (1925). Of these direct or indirect imitators of Cervantes, Herman Melville is undoubtedly the most faithful to his spirit. Yet *Moby Dick* (1853), for all its obvious echoes of *Don Quixote*, achieves something like a symmetrical reversal of its theme, pitching it in a heroic, tragi-comic key. Its narrator, Ishmael, quite the opposite of Cide Hamete Benengeli, is filled with Quixotic enthusiasm. His paean to the science of whales and the craft of whaling (Chapter 23) reveals the same passionate, punctilious, and bookish intimacy with his subject as the Don shows towards knight-errantry. He divides whales into folios, octavos, and duodecimos, and thence into chapters; he undertakes to break a lance in whalemen's honour, claiming that they liberated South America from the yoke of old Spain. His idealism perpetuates that of his former shipmates on the *Pequod; their* helmet of Mambrino is the gold Ecuadorian doubloon nailed to the mainmast in a spirit that is described as quintessentially poetic and Hispanic. Melville, in his private edition of *Don Quixote*, which he annotated in his own hand, warmly endorses what the hero has to say about chivalry's aims of liberty, justice, and equality, ignoring the contextual ironies of these speeches. In *Moby Dick*, the oceaning wanderings of the *Pequod*, captained by the monomaniac Captain Ahab and crewed by a sordid gang of savages and social outcasts, become a sort of latter-day crusade, and also a symbol of the common man's capacity to scale heights of heroism, idealism, and genius. In Chapter 26 they elicit a Whitmanesque hymn to the Spirit of Equality and God of Democracy: 'Thou who, in all Thy mighty, earthly marchings, ever callest Thy selectest champions from Thy kingly commons, bear me out in it, O God!' Cervantes, rubbing shoulders with Bunyan and Andrew Jackson, is amongst the elect. The primitive goodness buried in the soul of the common man is exemplified by the savage Queequeg – Sancho Panza of this novel; friendship with him enables Ishmael to overcome his sense of solitude. Concerning this crew of islanders, one thinks of Donne: 'No man is an island, entire of itself'. For Melville, as for many twentieth-century writers, including Unamuno, human solidarity is a salve for transcendental pessimism. His hero, Ahab, chasing after universal evil in the form of the White Whale, infuses a Quixotic sense of destiny with tragic Shakespearean frenzy; life's material flux, symbolised by the waves traversed by the *Pequod*, is a mere screen for transcendental ideas, or perhaps figments, that man is doomed to pursue, perishing in the attempt.

The direct influence of Cervantes in the twentieth century becomes more localised than in the preceding one; it is chiefly to be found in Spain, and, to a lesser extent, in Latin America. The canonisation of *Don Quixote* by the German Romantics was repeated, a century after the event, by the Spanish writers of the so-called generation of 1898, including the poet Antonio Machado and Unamuno. Allusions to Cervantes's novel, particularly his hero, pervade their poems, essays, fiction, and landscape-descriptions. Ortega y Gasset, who was junior to them, shared their esteem for Cervantes and their aspirations. They regarded *Don Quixote* as embodying the quintessence of the cultural values that they wished to re-generate in their own country. The book was an important source of evidence for Unamuno in his diagnosis of the traditionalist, oppositional mentality that Spain evolved in its imperial period (*On the Cult of Caste* [1895]). Ortega took it as the central illustration of his ideas in his first major work of philosophy – *Meditations on 'Don Quixote'* (1914). His theme is culture's function in human life and its need for constant renewal; his drift resembles Unamuno's in the essays just cited. That is, he invites the Spanish mind to show sympathetic curiosity to its immediate circumstances, and also to extend its intellectual horizons towards Europe. These two works have had a profound impact on the way in which Spaniards in this century have considered their history, including Spanish Golden Age culture and Cervantes's place in it. One example of this influence is Américo Castro's seminal book on the thought of Cervantes (1925); another, a major novel of the post-Civil War period, is Luis Martín Santos's *Time of Silence* (1961).

The great Argentine novelist, Jorge Luis Borges, has written essays on *Don Quixote* that attribute to it a Borgesian theme: man searching for transcendental meaning in mental and verbal labyrinths of his own making. One may therefore infer its influence on Borges's own fiction, including *Ficciones* (1944) and *El Aleph* (1949). The Mexican novelist Carlos Fuentes has insistently proclaimed allegiance to Cervantes on behalf of all Latin American literature; while this is more an article of faith than a descriptive statement, it clearly must apply to Fuentes's own novels: e.g. *Change of Skin* (1967).

Cervantine *aficionados* outside the Spanish-speaking world include Gide, Hašek, and Nabokov. Gide's *The Counterfeiters* (1926) has been described as 'a novel about a novelist writing a novel which invites the collaboration of its readers'; its loose yet intricate structure deliberately mirrors art's relation to the formless material offered by life. It joins the large self-conscious species which goes back to *Don Quixote* through *Tristram Shandy* (Alter 1975). The hero of Jaroslav Hašek's *The Good Soldier Švejk*, written just after the First World War, has become the legendary embodiment of the little man's means of self-defence against the bureaucratic or military machine: passive recalcitrance. Švejk, with his simulated imbecility, his directness, his cheerful equanimity, his anecdotal and discursive style, contains much of Sancho Panza. Vladimir Nabokov's Humbert Humbert and Charles Kimbote, of *Lolita* (1958) and *Pale Fire* (1962) respectively, are obvious descendants of the mad knight by virtue of their literary fixations, though their Dulcineas are startlingly different from his.

However, in general, the influence of Cervantes on the modern novel has become more diffuse and imprecise than it was previously. The reason for this is that the modernist revolution, associated with Proust, Joyce, Woolf, Faulkner, Mann, Kafka, and others, led novelists away from the Cervantine formula that their nineteenth-century precursors found so inspiring. New themes took its place: the sense of living in a world without gods and without a tradition-sanctioned culture; the turning in upon subjective consciousness and forms of mimesis based on its perspectives; the erosion of assumptions about the stable, objectively analysable nature of society and personality; the awareness of art's problematic relation to life; the glorification of the artist's power to achieve redemption through his illusions. To be sure, Cervantine critics since Américo Castro have insisted on Cervantes's role as inspired precursor of such themes; and their claims have been complemented by the thriving modern industry of theory and history of the novel: Lukács, Shklovsky, Bakhtin, Trilling, Levin, Marthe Robert, Girard, Wayne Booth, R. Alter, and others. So, Bakhtin's account (1981) of how, in the novel, the centrifugal forces of 'heteroglossia' (deviant discourse) subvert the 'monoglot' tendency to make language and ideology conform to an official standard, harmonises easily with the kind of approach to *Don Quixote* that was initiated by Américo Castro (see p. 2). Yet to judge by the testimony that matters most – that of conscious imitation by practising novelists – the critics and theorists have over-played their hand.

In most of the great modernists, the presence of *Don Quixote* lingers like an old perfume, vaguely discernible amongst other scents. I offer two examples. In Thomas Mann's fiction, from *Buddenbrooks* (1901) onwards, there is a constant, unresolved conflict between artistic imagination or Faustian intellectual curiosity, conceived as morbidly destructive, and the practical necessities of social life: making money, emotional attachments, the imperatives of humanist culture. Here we have a modern continuation of the theme of illusion's collision with reality, essential to the 'Cervantine formula' as the nineteenth century perceived it. Yet the chief roots of Mann's preoccupation are surely not to be found in *Don Quixote* but in nineteenth-century German culture: e.g. in Romanticism, Wagner, Nietzsche. In 1934, during a transatlantic voyage, Mann wrote a long, sympathetic, and intelligent essay on Cervantes's novel; it stops well short of confessions of indebtedness such as Flaubert's. Likewise, in James Joyce's *Ulysses* (1922), the traces of Cervantine perfume may be divined, yet defy precise indentification. Something like the opposition of Quixote and Sancho seems to recur in the pairing of Stephen Dedalus and Leopold Bloom. The former is a solitary, Icarus-like intellectual and artist; the latter is an Irish Jew, an advertising canvasser, and the epitome of the *homme moyen sensuel*. Their wanderings round Dublin in the course of an uneventful day evoke those of Telemachus and Ulysses, hence the mock-epic form of Quixote's adventures. Yet it is hardly necessary to insist, since Joyce's title makes the point implicitly, that the literary allusions of *Ulysses* are tantamount to the multitudinous chorus of Western European culture; Cervantes's voice is just one amongst many. Joyce could only be counted a follower of Cervantes if qualifications for entry to the club were made amorphously all-embracing. The same considerations apply, in general, to the post-modernists: the novelists who have plied their craft since the Second World War.

I return to the real *aficionados* in order to illustrate this century's updating of the Quixotic theme. It is interesting to compare Kafka with Unamuno in this respect, since they display a characteristically modern sense of paradox in ways that appear at first very unlike, but prove on closer inspection to be quite similar. In Kafka's *The Castle* (1926), a man called 'K', about whose previous existence we know nothing, arrives at a village under the jurisdiction of a castle. He believes that the authorities at the castle have appointed him as land-surveyor; this seems to be confirmed by two letters, an overheard telephone-conversation, and the arrival of two assistants who have been sent to help him in his work. Yet all his efforts to gain access to the castle's superintendent, Klamm, in order to confirm the appointment, end in failure; and he is eventually forced to yield to the villagers' incoherent yet immovable scepticism about his title to the post. There is a Kafkaesque paradox here: on the one hand, his status seems incontestable; on the other, the only means of proof lies with the villagers. There is moral paradox too: are the villagers to blame for their insubordinate scepticism, or is 'K' being obscurely punished for his obedience to the letter of authority's commands? The novel's affinities with *Don Quixote*, on which Marthe Robert (1977) has insisted, may be inferred from the enigmatic symbolism of the settings and characters: the castle evokes a Grail-like quest, or an interior castle; land-surveying is concerned with the identification of boundaries and property-rights; 'K' counts on his relation to Frieda – 'Peace' – to secure the desired interview with her ex-lover, Klamm, suggestive of pincers, oppressive silence. *The Castle*, like Kafka's other stories, is an ironic parable about – here one is seized by appropriate uncertainty – man's relation to the absolute. He is fated to seek it and be mocked by the quest, which merely leads to Kafka's famous blind-alleys and double binds.

Within the brief compass of *St Manuel Bueno, Martyr* (1931), Unamuno compresses the essence of his philosophy. The story develops a principal theme in Unamuno's commentary on *Don Quixote* (1905): namely, that Quixote's secret motive was exis-

tential anguish, which he sought to appease by the heroic buf-
foonery of chivalric altruism and devotion to Dulcinea: his
eternal Idea. The story is narrated by Angela Carballino; she is
prompted to make the confession because proceedings for the
beatification of Manuel Bueno are now in progress; her narrative
concerns the life and personality of the man who was, to her, a
cross between spiritual father and spiritual son. His ministry as
parish-priest of the village of Valverde de Lucerna was, in a literal
sense, Christ-like. Yet it concealed a dark, sacrilegious secret:
his selfless devotion to the spiritual welfare of his parishioners
was an attempt to still his own scepticism and conviction of life's
empty tedium; he nourished *their* ingenuous faith in order to
protect them from his own despair. Worst of all, Manuel Bueno
believed that this was Christ's secret too: hence, for him, the
poignant significance of the cry: 'My God, my God, why hast
thou forsaken me?' His ministry thus invests Marx's jibe about
religion – 'opium of the people' – with grim seriousness. Angela's
brother Lázaro, formerly anti-clerical, returns to the village, falls
under Manuel Bueno's spell, and is won over to his holy farce.
When Manuel Bueno administers the host to him at his first communion, it falls from his hand, and the cock crows. Eventually,
Manuel Bueno dies, venerated by his flock; after her brother's
death, Angela is left alone with her memories and her spiritual
torment. Angela's narrative tragically re-works the implications
of the traditional metaphor of the dream of life. Yet she, and
Unamuno through her, manage to derive consolation from the
metaphor's creative suggestions. May not Manuel Bueno's scepticism have been a form of faith? Was not the effect of his ministry
on his parishioners a more significant answer to that question
than his inner state of mind? The absurd wager on which
Unamuno stakes all is: man's hunger for the absolute creates the
absolute. The conclusion seems opposed to Kafka's. Yet Unamuno's creed lacks any trace of dogmatic certainty; as a wager, it is
qualified by a 'maybe', which is enveloped within layers of
'dream': Angela's subjective consciousness; the status of her
chronicle, dependent on other reports and, ultimately, on

Unamuno's fiction. We are back at Kafkaesque paradox, whose two sides both support and demolish each other. It was a form of irony that Cervantes never knew.

I began this chapter by alluding to the quest of relevance that motivates our interest in old books; neither the chapter nor this book should be interpreted as a futile plea for its abandonment. It is a potent force in advancing our understanding of the classics. Many of the critical concepts that we now have, and find indispensable for the discussion of *Don Quixote* – e.g. an individual writer's world-view, his handling of narrative viewpoint, his irony – were the discovery of generations who came after Cervantes; and the stimulus for discovery often consisted in artistic developments such as those discussed in this chapter. Thus, if it were not for Sterne, and the self-conscious tradition which followed him, it would scarcely occur to us to think of Cervantes as a self-conscious novelist; Sterne, we might say, has taught us to see aspects of *Don Quixote* that its contemporaries were not trained to perceive or rationalise. The quest for relevance only becomes excessive when the potentially anachronistic frame of reference of the questions that we put to the classics is allowed to dictate the nature of the answers. The controlling criterion of what the classics mean, and of whether we have understood, is the once-living hum of cultural implications that surrounded *them* and that they still implicitly contain. The criterion is not the loud buzz emanating from the culture that surrounds *us*. 'Understood' has a relative, not an absolute value; it is imaginative approximation, not certainty – unavailable in any kind of historical enquiry, however recent or remote its object. Yet the relativity of our understanding does not exempt it from judgements of greater or lesser validity. Why should these matter? Because the more we become dulled to that historic hum, the more we let the classics lose one of their essential claims on our curiosity, just as important as their relevance. I mean their difference. The word is not meant in a Derridean sense.

Guide to further reading

In drawing up this list I have borne the interests of non-Hispanists firmly in mind, though they are not my exclusive consideration. Since critical commentary on *Don Quixote* is, to put it mildly, prolific, the list is drastically selective.

The best handy modern edition of *Don Quixote* is by Luis Andrés Murillo (2 vols., Madrid, 1978), which synthesises in its notes the accumulated wisdom of two centuries of editorial work on Cervantes's novel. Diego Clemencín's edition (6 vols., Madrid, 1833–39) remains indispensable for its documentation of Cervantes's parodic allusions to romances of chivalry, and F. Rodríguez Marín's (10 vols., Madrid, 1947–49) is helpful for its elucidation of Golden Age usage. John Ormsby's translation of *Don Quixote* (1885, revised and re-edited by J.R. Jones and K. Douglas, New York, 1981) is the most reliable version in English; J.M. Cohen's workmanlike and somewhat looser translation is readily available (Penguin, Harmondsworth, 1967).

Melveena McKendrick's biography, *Cervantes* (Boston, Mass., 1980), treats its subject lucidly and reliably; E.C. Riley's book, *Don Quixote* (London, 1986), is an excellent general survey of the novel's salient aspects; it balances above the swirling cross-currents of contemporary *Quixote* criticism and offers a clear chart of them in its bibliography. P.E. Russell's *Cervantes* (Oxford, 1985), also authoritative, is brief, hence more general in its approach than Riley's. Martín de Riquer's *Aproximación al 'Quijote'* (Madrid, 1967), is informative about sixteenth- century opposition to novels of chivalry (*cf.* his 'Cervantes y la caballeresca' in *Suma Cervantina* [below]), but otherwise its exposition is somewhat dry and elementary.

It is difficult to recommend a single book which gives a good, up-to-date study of Cervantes's works as a whole. *Suma Cervantina*, ed. J.B. Avalle Arce and E.C. Riley (London, 1973), is a collection of essays (in Spanish) by leading authorities on Cervantes covering all the main aspects of his writings; the essays are variable in quality and sometimes idiosyncratic in approach. They may be supplemented by A.K. Forcione, *Cervantes' Christian Romance: A Study of 'Persiles y Sigismunda'* (Princeton, NJ, 1972); E.H. Friedman, *The Unifying Concept: Approaches to the Structure of Cervantes' 'Comedias'* (York, South Carolina, 1981); Ruth El Saffar, *Novel to Romance: A Study of Cervantes' 'Novelas ejemplares'* (Baltimore, 1974). J. Casalduero's series of commentaries on the 'sense and form' of Cervantes's major works, save *La Galatea,* are still worth consulting for their freshness and critical intelligence. Each title begins *Sentido y forma de.* . .. The book on *Don Quixote* (Madrid, 1949) has aged less well than those on the *Novelas* (Buenos Aires, 1943), *Persiles* (Buenos Aires, 1947), and the theatre (Madrid, 1951). General essays on the history and culture of the Spanish Golden Age are included in *Spain: A Companion to Spanish Studies*, ed. P.E. Russell (Oxford, 1973); they help to set Cervantes in a broad contemporary context.

Useful brief summaries of *Quixote* criticism are contained in Dana B. Drake, *Don Quijote (1894–1970): A Selective Annotated Bibliography* I (Chapel Hill, NC, 1974), II (Miami, Florida, 1978), III (New York, 1980). Also worth consulting is Luis Murillo's selective *Bibliografía fundamental*, the third volume of his edition of *Don Quixote* (cited above). There are two periodical publications dedicated exclusively to Cervantes: *Cervantes* (1981–   ) and *Anales Cervantinos* (1951–   ).

Besides *Suma Cervantina*, the collections of critical essays on Cervantes include: *Cervantes*, ed. Lowry Nelson Jr. (Englewood Cliffs, NJ, 1969); *Critical Essays on Cervantes*, ed. Ruth El Saffar (Boston, Mass., 1986); *El 'Quijote' de Cervantes*, ed. G. Haley (Madrid, 1984); *The Anatomy of 'Don Quixote', a symposium*, ed. M.J. Benardete and A. Flores (second edition, New York, 1969). Several of the essays cited in this book are anthologised in them. Non-Hispanists may obtain a conspectus of Américo Castro's evolving interpretations of Cervantes from *An Idea of History: Selected Essays of Américo Castro*, translated and edited by S. Gilman and E.L. King (Columbus, Ohio, 1977).

It is difficult to cite a study of Cervantes's ideology which has not some particular axe to grind. With that proviso, I mention: Américo Castro, *El pensamiento de Cervantes* (Madrid, 1925; re-edited 1972) and *Hacia Cervantes* (third edition, Madrid, 1967); Marcel Bataillon, *Erasmo y España* (Mexico, 1950; original French version, 1937), final chapter; F. Márquez Villanueva, *Fuentes literarias cervantinas* (Madrid, 1973) and *Personajes y temas del 'Quijote'* (Madrid, 1975); J.A. Maravall, *Utopía y contrautopía en el 'Quijote'* (Santiago de Compostela, 1976); A.K. Forcione, *Cervantes and the Humanist Vision* (Princeton, NJ, 1982).

The following studies have established themselves over the years as being particularly informative on some specific aspect of Cervantes's art, thought, or background: Henry Thomas, *Spanish and Portuguese Romances of Chivalry* (Cambridge, 1920); E.C. Riley, *Cervantes's Theory of the Novel* (Oxford, 1962); A. Rosenblat, *La lengua del 'Quijote'* (Madrid, 1971); R. Flores, *The Compositors of the First and Second Madrid Editions of 'Don Quixote' Part I* (London, 1975): G. Stagg, 'Revision in *Don Quijote* Part I', in *Hispanic Studies in Honour of Ignacio González Llubera* (Oxford, 1959), 347–66; L.A. Murillo, *The Golden Dial: Temporal Configuration in 'Don Quijote'* (Oxford, 1975); P.E. Russell, '*Don Quixote* as a Funny Book', *Modern Language Review* 64 (1969), 312–26.

My own book, *The Romantic Approach to 'Don Quixote'* (Cambridge, 1978), is a critical history of 'Quixote' criticism since 1800 and of the influence upon it of the modern age's myths about Cervantes. Other works concerned with the reception of Cervantes in the modern era, including his influence on the modern novel, include: Harry Levin, 'The Example of Cervantes' and 'Cervantes and *Moby Dick*', in *Contexts of Criticism* (Harvard University Press, 1957); Stuart Tave, *The Amiable Humorist*

(University of Chicago, 1960): Lionel Trilling, 'Manners, Morals, and the Novel' in *The Liberal Imagination* (London, 1961): René Girard, *Deceit, Desire, and the Novel* (Baltimore, 1965); Robert Alter, *Partial Magic: The Novel as a Self-Conscious Genre* (Berkeley, California, 1975); Marthe Robert, *The Old and the New: From Don Quixote to Kafka* (Berkeley, California, 1977); M. Bakhtin, *The Dialogic Imagination*, ed. M. Holquist (Austin, Texas, 1981).

I list without further comment the critical works, apart from those mentioned above, which have been cited in the course of this study:

E. Auerbach, 'The Enchanted Dulcinea' in *Mimesis. The Representation of Reality in Western Literature* (Princeton, NJ, 1953), 293–315

H. Bergson, *Laughter. An Essay on the Meaning of the Comic* (London, 1913)

E.M. Forster, *Aspects of the Novel* (London, 1961)

M. Foucault, *The Order of Things* (New York, 1970), Chapter 2

Mia Gerhardt, *'Don Quijote'; la vie et les livres* (Amsterdam, 1955)

O.H. Green, 'El ingenioso hidalgo' in *The Literary Mind of Medieval and Renaissance Spain* (Lexington, Kentucky, 1970), 171–84.

Erich Heller, *The Disinherited Mind* (Cambridge, 1952)

M. Joly, *La Bourle et son interprétation (Espagne, XVIe–XVIIe siècles)* (Atelier National Reproduction des Thèses, Université de Lille III, 1981)

S. de Madariaga, *'Don Quixote': An Introductory Essay in Psychology* (revised edition, London, 1961)

O. Mandel, 'The Function of the Norm in *Don Quixote*', *Modern Philology* 55 (1957–58), 154–63

Thomas Mann, 'Voyage with *Don Quixote*' in *Cervantes*, ed. Lowry Nelson Jr, 49–72 (see above)

M. Menéndez Pelayo, 'Cultura literaria de Miguel de Cervantes y elaboración del "Quijote"' (lecture of 1905) in *San*

Isidoro, Cervantes, y otros estudios (Austral edition, Buenos Aires, 1947), 75–126

R. Menéndez Pidal, 'Un aspecto en la elaboración del *Quijote*' (lecture, 1920), in *De Cervantes y Lope de Vega* (Austral edition, Buenos Aires, 1948), 9–56

J.F. Montesinos, 'Algunas reflexiones sobre la figura del donaire en el teatro de Lope de Vega' in *Homenaje a Menéndez Pidal*, 3 vols. (Madrid, 1925), I, 469–504

J. Ortega y Gasset, *Meditaciones del 'Quijote'* ([1914] second edition, Madrid, 1921)

A.A. Parker, 'Fielding and the Structure of *Don Quixote*', *Bulletin of Hispanic Studies* 33 (1956), 1–16

The Philosophy of Love in Spanish Literature (Edinburgh, 1985)

H. Percas de Ponsetti, *Cervantes y su concepto del arte,* 2 vols. (Madrid, 1975)

R. Poggioli, *The Oaten Flute: Essays on the Pastoral and the Pastoral Ideal* (Harvard University Press, 1975), chapters 7 and 8

A. Redondo, 'Tradición carnavalesca y creación literaria del personaje de Sancho Panza. . .', *Bulletin Hispanique*, 80 (1978), 39–70

L. Spitzer, 'Linguistic Perspectivism in the *Don Quijote*' in *Linguistics and Literary History* (Princeton, NJ, 1948), 41–85

Miguel de Unamuno, *Vida de Don Quijote y Sancho* ([1905] Austral edition, Buenos Aires, 1946)

DATE DUE
